BY LESLIE HASKER

FULHAM AND HAMMERSMITH HISTORICAL SOCIETY

First published 1984
© Leslie F Hasker, 1984

2nd Impression 2005
Published by
The Fulham & Hammersmith Historical Society
Flat 12
43 Peterborough Road,
London SW6 3BT

All Rights Reserved.

No part of this publication may be reproduced, stored in a retrieval system, or transmitted in any form whatsoever, electronic, photocopying, recording or otherwise, without the prior permission of the publishers.

ISBN 09016 42-20-7

Printed by The Alden Group Ltd, Oxford.

Cover Picture
This shows a programme produced for one of the local national savings weeks organized periodically throughout the War. 'Salute the Soldier Week' produced nearly one million pounds in Fulham.
(Courtesy Hammersmith and Fulham Public Libraries)

CONTENTS

CHAPTER ONE
YEARS OF UNEASY PEACE — 9

CHAPTER TWO
FROM MUNICH TO WAR — 18

CHAPTER THREE
TWILIGHT WAR TO REAL WAR — 26

CHAPTER FOUR
THE BLITZ: SEPTEMBER 1940-DECEMBER 1940 — 37

CHAPTER FIVE
THE BLITZ: DECEMBER 1940-MAY 1941 — 47

CHAPTER SIX
HOLDING ON: MAY 1941-DECEMBER 1941 — 53

CHAPTER SEVEN
WORLD WAR: JANUARY 1942-DECEMBER 1942 — 60

CHAPTER EIGHT
WAITING FOR D-DAY: JANUARY 1943-JUNE 1944 — 68

CHAPTER NINE
D-DAY AND AFTER: JUNE 1944-AUGUST 1945 — 78

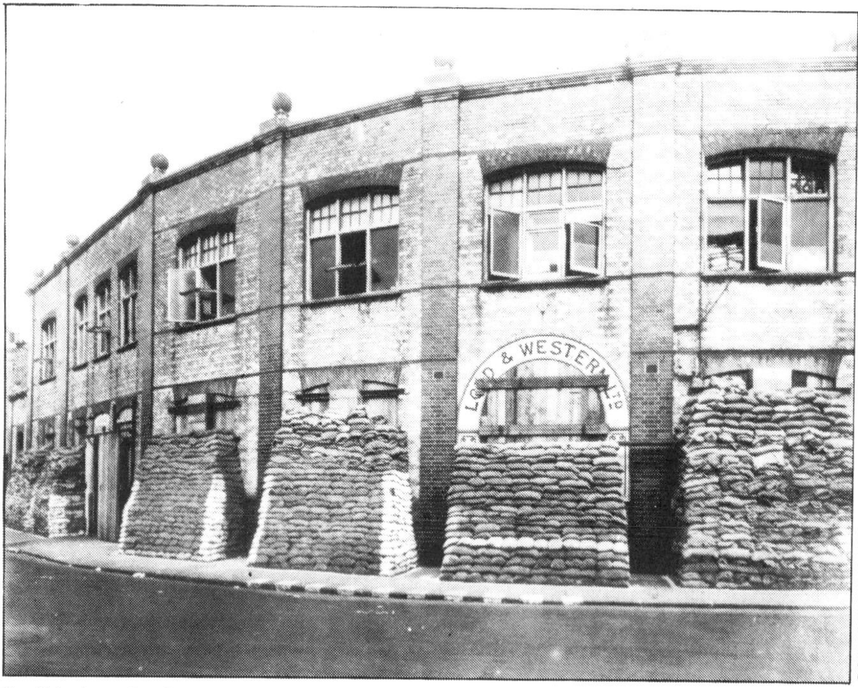

COURTESY NATIONAL SUNLIGHT LAUNDRIES

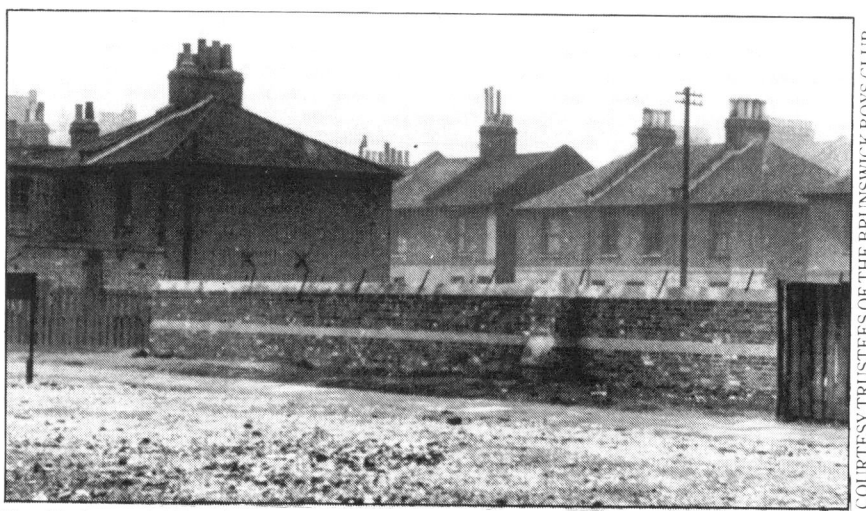

Sunlight Laundry, Broughton Road. Sandbagged because it was to be a cleansing station for use after poison gas attacks.

COURTESY TRUSTEES OF THE BRUNSWICK BOYS CLUB

Site of the Brunswick Boys Club, Haldane Road, 1946. The largest surface air raid shelter in Fulham was built here. It had been cleared away when this photograph was taken, but a large brick-built water tank for fire-fighting still remained.

INTRODUCTION

SOME years ago I wrote a book entitled 'The Place Which is Called Fulanham': an outline history of Fulham from Roman times until the start of the Second World War. The book was published in 1981. It did not deal with the Second World War because the years 1939-45 seemed to merit a separate and more detailed study. They were remarkable years during which many old people in Fulham became more familiar with the frightening crash of high explosives than their uniformed grandsons away in the armed forces.

Very few accounts have been written of specific parts of London during 1939-45. So far as I can ascertain, those that have appeared were all published during the immediate post-war years. The perspective of events has now changed. I have relied largely on official records for the basic facts, and have also gathered items of information from people who were in Fulham during the War. A good deal of interest has been shown in the background events of everyday life such as food rationing. This and other subsidiary matters have been dealt with in the book.

I wish to record my appreciation of the help given by the Archivist of the London Borough of Hammersmith and Fulham, Chris Jeens, in using the official records; and of Christine Bayliss, the local history assistant at Fulham Library, for help in using the extensive Fulham local history collection at Fulham Library. I have also made good use of the reference department at Hammersmith Central Library, and must thank the reference librarian Peter Jackaman for his help. The staff of the Public Record Office at Kew have also been most helpful. My thanks also to the various Fulham people who have supplied me with information on aspects of the War.

LESLIE HASKER

Fulham Hospital after bombing, September 1940.

CHAPTER ONE

YEARS OF UNEASY PEACE

WHEN the bombers came to Fulham, it was the Borough's Civil Defence Services which had to cope with the immediate effect of the attacks. Yet those Services had been formed only three years before the War, and were developed in the face of general public apathy and much outright opposition. There was a considerable pacifist feeling in Britain between the two World Wars resulting from the dreadful casualties of 1914-18.

From the early nineteen-twenties onwards, experts had been studying the likely effects of air raids in any future conflict. The Air Marshals had advised that each ton of bombs dropped would cause fifty casualties, and that one third of the casualties would be fatal. London was expected to be the main target. Casualties in the capital were likely to be 1700 killed in the first twenty-four hours and 1275 in the second twenty-four hours. After that, 850 people would be killed every twenty-four hours for a month. Experience was to show that these forecasts were greatly exaggerated, but they were expert assessments and at the time were accepted as such. Plans had to be worked out for the various services that would be needed to cope with the effects of bombing. It was decided that the local authorities should be assigned responsibility for organising Air Raid Precautions (A.R.P.) in their areas. Because of the national mood in the immediate pre-war years, many difficulties had to be overcome.

In April 1935 an Air Raid Precautions Department of the Home Office was established with responsibility for supervising the development of A.R.P. In July the Home Office issued its first A.R.P. Circular to all local authorities. The Circular, and two subsequent letters, stated that a conference was to be held in London in October to explain the organization proposed for Air Raid Precautions. Fulham Borough Council was invited to send representatives. The Circular was referred to the Law and Parliamentary Committee, and was considered by the Committee at its meeting in September. After careful consideration, Alderman Harold Laski, who was a member of the Committee and a Professor at the London School of Economics, moved a resolution agreeing that representatives be sent. But the resolution went on to say . . . 'at the same time the Home Office be informed that this Council consider that the action suggested in their circular in the event of a mass air raid would be futile and ineffective; that the Council believes that the mere publication of the document is conducive to the creation of a war mentality and a demand for increased armaments, and was actually issued by the Government in order to obtain the support of public opinion for its dangerous policy of trebling the

Air Force; that the Council understands that all expert opinion has declared that there can be no real protection of the civil population against air raids, and that it therefore calls upon the Government to withdraw the circular and concentrate its energies upon the maintenance of peace.' The length and detail of this resolution suggests that it was drawn up before the meeting of the Committee.

The next development in Fulham came in March 1936 when the Law and Parliamentary Committee considered new Circulars and memoranda from the Home Office. These gave guidance on the setting up of local A.R.P. services, and information on anti-gas training and decontamination. The Committee decided to recommend to the Borough Council that an A.R.P. Committee should be established, but that the Council should decline to take any part in creating a civilian force for defence in war-time. One factor influencing this decision was that the Government was not prepared to make a financial contribution to local authorities to help with their expenses in the field of A.R.P. At the full meeting of the Council in April there came a remarkable turnabout. The Chairman of the Law and Parliamentary Committee withdrew his Committee's recommendation, and substituted a new one that a Committee of six should be formed to investigate and report on Borough services in the event of air raids. The changed recommendation was approved by the Borough Council. There was obviously a deep division of opinion among the Councillors. In the municipal elections held the previous November the Labour Party had gained control of Fulham Borough Council for the first time since 1922. International developments may have influenced opinions concerning Air Raid Precautions because on 7 March 1936 Hitler had ordered German troops to march into the Rhineland. This area had been demilitarized by the Treaty of Versailles. In Britain the general reaction had been 'it's German territory so let them get on with it', but Hitler's action was a clear demonstration of his growing confidence.

On September 9 the new Fulham A.R.P. Committee held its first meeting under the chairmanship of Councillor da Palma. The summer had been an uneasy one. The Italians had invaded Abyssinia in October 1935, and had achieved victory by the following May. In July 1936 Spain had been plunged into civil war. With this worrying background, work had been going on concerning the allocation of air raid responsibilities among the Council departments. This was in accordance with the outline plans for dealing with air raids which had been issued by the Home Office.

The Borough Engineer would be responsible for work on damaged buildings, the rescue of people trapped inside them, the repair of roads, etc. The Medical Officer of Health would organize first aid parties to collect injured people and take them to the first aid posts. Those needing further medical treatment would be taken on to Fulham Hospital, sited where Charing Cross Hospital was later built. The huge power station in Townmead Road, of which the first section had just been opened, was controlled by Fulham Borough Council. It supplied electricity over much of Greater London. Plans had to be made to keep it operating, for power stations were sure to be prime bombing targets. The Town Clerk would be responsible for the enrolment of the many volunteers likely to be needed. Somewhere in the Town Hall a control centre would have to be set up to direct operations during air raids. The officials concerned had acquired substantial new responsibilities added to their normal work.

Two days before Christmas 1936 the A.R.P. Committee met again, this time with a representative from the A.R.P. Department of the Home Office in attendance. He must have been urging more progress, because at the end of the meeting it was agreed to proceed with the appointment of a full-time A.R.P. organizer. There were opposing views on this matter because of the continuing refusal of the Government to give any financial help, and the decision was carried only by the casting vote of the Chairman, Councillor da Palma. This man seems to have been the decisive influence in driving forward preparations to deal with bombing in Fulham. In February 1937 the A.R.P. Committee met to consider a letter from the Home Office complaining of a lack of progress in preparing for possible air raids. The letter said that twenty-four of the twenty-eight Boroughs in London were making good progress, but four others including Fulham had done little.

In March 1937 the House of Commons was informed that an Air Raid Wardens service was to be established. This development was influenced by the organization in Germany of a similar system of 'House Wardens'. A Warden should be a responsible member of the public, chosen to be a leader and adviser of his neighbours, and he would operate from a Warden's Post. During air raids he would telephone reports to the control centre on the fall of bombs giving details of damage. Men over thirty years of age were to be preferred as Wardens, and there was no reason why women should not be enrolled. This scheme provided civil defence with what turned out to be its most distinctive institution, and one which stood up well to the test of hard experience. Following the Parliamentary announcement the Home Secretary broadcast an appeal for volunteers as Wardens. The broadcast was made at a relatively unimportant time, and there was little public response.

Meanwhile, millions of sandbags were ordered to protect key buildings against high explosive bombs. The production of gas masks was increased, and large supplies of medical equipment and other items were ordered. All this material was being paid for by the Government for eventual free issue to local authorities.

Politically-conscious people were increasingly concerned by developments in Spain, some going so far as to say that the Spanish Civil War was the scenario for a general European conflict. German Air Force units sent to help General Franco were gaining valuable operational experience. A Home Office official was sent to Madrid to study the effects of bombing.

The King's Speech at the opening of the new Parliamentary session in October 1937 included the statement 'My ministers are anxious that energetic steps shall be taken to complete the measures for the protection of the civilian population against aid raids.' Just before Christmas an Air Raid Precautions Act became law, bringing to a close two and a half years of voluntary effort on the part of local authorities. The Act required them to prepare local A.R.P. schemes based on guidance from the Home Office. The other change of major importance was that the Government would reimburse local authorities with approximately eighty per cent of their A.R.P. expenditure.

The difficulty over financial liability had delayed developments in London concerning fire-fighting. The Germans had developed a very effective incendiary bomb before the end of the First World War. This was a one kilogram magnesium cylinder with a thermite core which ignited and burnt fiercely for three or four minutes. These incendiaries could be carried in considerable numbers by bombers. The A.R.P. planners judged correctly that incendiary bombs were likely to be used on a large scale, and they could break through roofs and cause many fires. A major expansion of the fire services would therefore be needed in the event of war.

In February 1937 the Government sent a Circular to all fire authorities informing them of the problem. Plans would need to be prepared for a ten-fold increase in fire-fighting personnel and equipment. The Government Circular was purely advisory, and at that time there was no compulsion to act. Fulham fire station in Fulham Road formed part of the London County Council fire brigade. At first the L.C.C. refused to take any action that would involve expenditure because the Government was not prepared to meet any of the costs.

In November, Fulham's A.R.P. Committee received a report from a member of the Medical Officer's staff who had completed a course of training at the Falfield anti-gas school in Gloucestershire. The Committee decided to arrange lectures in the Town Hall for local doctors and nurses concerning poison gas, but it was obviously necessary to have more staff trained in the subject. There was a waiting list for the anti-gas school, and the Committee agreed to write to the A.R.P. Department of the Home Office urging the necessity for increased anti-gas training facilities. This was a complete change of attitude from that of only a year before when the appointment of an A.R.P. officer had been agreed only by the casting vote of the Chairman. The change reflected new thinking throughout the country. More and more people were beginning to feel that Hitler's Germany was a growing threat, and that Britain must strengthen the armed forces.

On 7 March 1938 the A.R.P. Committee met again. By then, planning of Fulham's war-time organization was beginning to produce detailed schemes. The A.R.P. control for the whole Borough was to be in the Town Hall, the Central First Aid Station would be in the Public Baths at Walham Green, and the Instruction Centre for the large number of volunteers required would be in the former maternity home at 706 Fulham Road. This had been replaced by a newly-built Maternity and Child Welfare Centre at Parsons Green, opened the previous October. The Council's Munster Road Depot would be the main base for rescue and repair parties to go to bomb-damaged houses, and also for road repairs, decontamination after poison gas attack, etc. The rescue parties would be made up of men with experience in building work, who could go into a badly damaged house and know what could be moved with safety. Rescue parties were recruited and controlled by the L.C.C. Some decentralization of these services was visualised, and the following places were suggested: Swan Wharf, Star Road Depot, Cassidy Road Depot, South Park and the Coroner's Court in Munster Road. It was estimated that four hundred people would be needed to provide round-the-clock cover at the centres chosen.

The organization of the A.R.P. Wardens was to be based on the polling districts, and there would be one Head Warden for each district. Sands End East and Sands End South would be excluded from the scheme. The Power Station in Townmead Road and the Gas Works at Sands End were likely to be important bombing targets, and the Committee felt that the entire community in the locality would have to be evacuated. During air raids two A.R.P. Wardens would be on duty at each post, plus one in reserve. It was thought that one thousand Wardens would need to be recruited and trained. The size of the recruiting problem facing Fulham was now becoming apparent and the picture was not yet complete. These A.R.P. plans were not hard and fast. In the course of time there were many changes. In the same month that Fulham's A.R.P. Committee was agreeing outline plans for its services, the London County Council completed its scheme to expand the fire service. Thirty thousand volunteer auxiliary firemen would be needed, as well as a large amount of additional equipment.

In March 1938 Hitler made another important move. He had been having discussions with the Chancellor of Austria concerning an economic union of their two countries, but the talks did not progress as Hitler had hoped. On March 12 German armed forces entered Austria, and three days later Hitler made a ceremonial entry into Vienna. The most important pictorial news in those days were the cinema newsreels which always preceded the main film. Nearly half the population went to the cinema at least once a week. The sight of the massed formations of jack-booted German troops marching into Vienna was a chilling experience.

On 20 June 1938 the A.R.P. Committee met to consider a range of reports on the development of A.R.P. services. It was then decided that the Borough should be divided into five divisions, each containing thirty-seven Air Raid Wardens area sectors. The notion that the southern part of Sands End would have to be completely evacuated had now been abandoned. Each area sector would be divided into individual Warden sectors. Although many volunteers were attending instruction classes in Wardens duties, more volunteers were needed. It was reported that A.R.P. recruitment nationally was not going well. People were most reluctant to believe in the probability of another war.

Notification had been received from the Home Office that a Grand Council under the name of Women's Voluntary Services had been formed by a nucleus of representatives of women's organizations. The W.V.S. was willing to help local authorities with A.R.P. work. On July 7 the W.V.S. held a public meeting in the Large Hall of Fulham Town Hall to explain their objectives. The Hall was packed, and one thousand membership application forms were issued. Only a few of these forms were subsequently completed and returned.

The Home Secretary had studied reports on the effects of bombing in Spain and had personally interviewed the Mayor of Barcelona, a town which had been heavily bombed. As a result the Government was asking local authorities to survey their areas and see which places could be adapted as shelters against bomb splinters and blast. This seems to have been the first time in which attention was focused on protection of the civilian population from high explosive bombs. The Government's basic policy was that there should be the maximum dispersal of population from

London and other large cities. This was the German policy, and the Germans were said to be well ahead of other countries in their A.R.P. preparations. It had been decided that air raid warnings would be by means of sirens operated by the police. The warning of approaching enemy aircraft would be a rising and falling note sounding for two minutes. The all clear would be a continuous steady sound, also for two minutes.

Fulham's Medical Officer of Health had given further consideration to the question of casualty services, and it was recommended that there should be three large First Aid Posts. They would be at Fulham Baths, Cobbs Hall in Fulham Palace Road, and in part of West Kensington Central School. This latter became Mary Boon School in 1959-60. Smaller First Aid Posts were contemplated for the Borough Council's Dispensary at 114 New Kings Road and their Clinic at 170 Wandsworth Bridge Road. These plans were tentative.

Huge numbers of civilian gas masks had been manufactured, and the Home Office was anxious to get these distributed to local authorities by the end of August. Fulham would be supplied with 150,000 gas masks. They would arrive in parts to be assembled locally in any factories where 'nimble fingered' work was done. This operation was said to be quite simple. If distribution to the public should be ordered, this would best be done by Air Raid Wardens working at schools or institutions. The gas masks came in a number of sizes because close fitting was essential when they were worn. The Home Office would need to know the numbers required for men and women, for children aged between five and sixteen, and between two and four. The design of a gas mask suitable for babies was proving difficult. Forced breathing is necessary when wearing a mask, and a baby could not breathe if wearing a standard type of mask. One suitable for babies had not been developed, but experiments were still going on. It was recommended that Air Raid Wardens should ascertain the numbers and sizes of masks required by means of house-to-house visits. The problem was that Fulham, in common with all other boroughs, had nothing like enough Wardens to do all this work.

The London Fire Service was also facing problems. Large numbers of trailer pumps and other necessary equipment such as hoses had been ordered, but a broadcast in June appealing for volunteers to train as auxiliary firemen brought only a limited response. An expert report early in 1938 calculated that a single bomber operating over a fairly closely populated area could start something like seventy-five fires. In a congested area, defined as one thirty per cent built over, the number of fires would be doubled. There was therefore considerable concern over the shortfall in volunteers for the Auxiliary Fire Service in London.

The European situation in general was deteriorating. In Spain the civil war dragged on, with both Germany and Italy increasing their help to General Franco. Czechoslovakia was an even greater worry. This republic had been established in 1918 from former provinces of Austria-Hungary. It comprised various races including some three million Germans in the Sudetenland part of the country. Immediately after the German union with Austria in March 1938, the Sudeten Germans began demanding autonomy. In May the Czech Government became worried by German troop movements near their frontier, and mobilized part of their forces. This tense situation continued throughout the summer.

The estimates of the British Air Staff concerning the growing strength of the German Air Force resulted in a continuous updating of the likely casualty figures if war were to come. The basic assessment remained unchanged. A war would start with a massive attack on London. This would be followed by daily bombing for the next sixty days. The follow-up bombing would spread to other towns and ports, but London would remain the prime target. By the end of this two months of bombing, six hundred thousand people would have been killed and twice as many injured.

It is now known that the Germans did not in fact have the capability to sustain such a massive aerial onslaught. Winston Churchill later said that, in those pre-war years, governments had been greatly misled by the 'expert' forecasts of devastation from bombing. He wrote: 'This picture of aerial destruction was so exaggerated that it depressed the statesmen responsible for the pre-war policy, and played a definite part in the desertion of Czecho-Slovakia in August 1938.'

The Ministry of Health had the responsibility of planning for the care of the huge number of casualties expected and at one time questioned whether it would be possible to continue such a war. However, preparations had to be made, and by the summer of 1938 a scheme was evolving for London. In the event of war all the hospitals in the metropolis would be cleared of as many patients as possible. The less ill would be sent home, and most of the remainder transferred to hospitals outside London. The largely-emptied hospitals would then await air raid casualties.

A survey of hospital resources outside the large towns showed them to be generally very inadequate. Many emergency single-storey hospitals were subsequently built in country areas to accommodate people injured in air raids. These hospitals have generally remained in use during the post-War years, often with later extensions.

At the beginning of 1938 the Government finally agreed, on the pressing advice of the Air Ministry, that a complete blackout would be necessary at night in wartime. There would be no street lighting. All premises would need to have their windows covered in such a way that no light could be seen outside.

By the end of June, regular returns from the local authorities were providing accurate figures concerning A.R.P. recruitment. In the London area, where rather more than one hundred thousand volunteers were needed, only forty thousand had been enrolled. Twenty-six thousand of these had been trained or were receiving training. In Fulham twelve hundred had been enrolled but a total of four thousand were needed. Clearly much remained to be done, and the Government decided on a new recruiting drive to start at the end of the holiday season.

One area in which a valuable advance was made during 1938 was the discovery that a fine spray of water would quickly extinguish a magnesium incendiary bomb. A small hand pump was then designed to direct such a spray, and large numbers of these pumps were ordered. They were fitted with a foot support something like a stirrup, and became known as stirrup pumps.

Throughout the summer intensive preparations continued in Fulham. The empty premises of the Consolidated Pneumatic Tool Company at 104 Lillie Road were leased for the storage of respirators, protective clothing against poison gas, and sandbags. Large supplies of these items began to arrive for stock. Numerous training classes for volunteers were being held, but more volunteers were still needed. Fulham's Medical Officer was worried by the inadequate number of volunteers for first aid work. There were not enough of them to man the projected main First Aid Post at Fulham Baths, still less the other posts. More Wardens were still urgently needed.

Meanwhile, there were further worrying developments in Europe. The leaders of the German minority in Czechoslovakia were demanding autonomy and union with Germany. The Czech Government resisted this demand which seemed likely to lead to the break-up of their twenty-year-old state. In August the German army began manoeuvres near the Czecho-Slovak border. On September 13 Hitler made a speech in which, referring to Czechoslovakia, he said he could not restrain his people any longer. There was now widespread alarm. Suddenly there came the sensational news that Neville Chamberlain had decided to fly to Germany and meet Hitler. It was a most surprising development but was welcomed by everybody. In those days leading statesmen did not fly.

Mr Chamberlain returned to London with proposals worked out at Berchtesgaden. These were discussed with the French leaders, and eventually agreement was reached. The Czech Government had little option but to accept the Anglo-French proposals, which were that any of their territory where the population was more than fifty per cent German should be transferred to Germany.

On September 22 Chamberlain again flew to Germany, this time to settle final details. To his great surprise, Hitler had now increased his demands. He wanted the Sudetenland placed under immediate German military occupation. The British Prime Minister flew back to London on Saturday September 24, grim and despondent. Defensive measures were immediately intensified. The Home Office sent instructions to the local authorities the same day telling them to assemble gas masks for distribution, dig shelter trenches in public open spaces and prepare first aid posts. On Monday the Observer Corps and the anti-aircraft units of the Territorial Army were called out.

In Fulham, as everywhere else in London, there began a frantic rush to prepare for air raids. Gas masks were rapidly assembled in local factories. A printed leaflet headed 'Distribution of Civilian Respirators Will Begin Immediately' was delivered to every house in Fulham. Local boy scouts gave a great deal of assistance in getting the leaflets distributed. The issue of gas masks was mainly from local schools, and people needed no urging to collect a mask. The original intention that trained Air Raid Wardens would see to the fitting and issue of masks was impracticable. The shortage of volunteers had resulted in there being nothing like enough Wardens, and a variety of willing helpers had to be found. Some problems arose. There were not enough small and medium sized masks, but there was a surplus of large masks. This situation was general throughout the country. The provision of masks for small children and babies presented many difficulties. A satisfactory 'baby-bag' had been finally designed and tested just before the Sudetenland crisis, but very few had been made. The 'baby-bag' had to be fitted over the baby's head and shoulders, and filtered air would be steadily pumped in by somebody using a bellows pump. The lack of these 'baby-bags' caused deep concern throughout Britain. Some parents caused angry scenes in Fulham Town Hall, and one man had to be arrested and taken before the magistrates. Needless to say none of the complainants had ever answered the repeated calls for volunteers for the A.R.P. services.

The digging of shelter trenches went on throughout the weekend. Arrangements were made for Messrs. Wimpey of Hammersmith to do this work on the Lillie Road Recreation Ground and on Eelbrook Common. The Borough Council's own labour force dug trenches in South Park. The new Maternity Centre at Parsons Green was closed and made ready for air raid casualties. Fulham Hospital prepared to remove as many patients as possible to make room for air raid casualties. At Fulham Baths work went on throughout Saturday night to floor over the mixed swimming pool. This was the first step towards establishing a First Aid Post there. All spare accommodation at the Mortuary and the Coroner's Court was cleared ready for bodies. Sandbags were filled and piled around key points. A detachment of troops moved into the Power Station in Townmead Road and set up machine guns on the roof ready to deal with low-flying aircraft. With hindsight, this was a futile precaution but then nobody knew quite what to expect.

There was a rush of new volunteers for Fulham's A.R.P. services. Army and R.A.F. recruiting offices were extremely busy, as also were the registrars of marriage. Many couples wanted to marry before the apparently inevitable war. Heavy traffic was reported on the roads out of London as people headed for safe places. North Wales was a favourite destination because it was felt that bombers could not operate among the mountains. Devonshire was the other favourite safe area.

On Wednesday September 28 the Fleet was mobilised. On the same day the House of Commons reassembled to hear the Prime Minister describe his negotiations with Hitler. While he was speaking a message arrived to say that Hitler had agreed to a four-power conference in Munich. Chamberlain, Daladier, Hitler and Mussolini met the next day, and shortly after midnight an agreement was signed stating that Germany would be allowed to occupy the Sudeten territories immediately. Once again the Czechs had little option but to agree.

CHAPTER TWO

FROM MUNICH TO WAR

THE Munich agreement brought a feeling of deep relief everywhere, for the nation had suffered a bad fright. Nevertheless, some people were highly critical of the settlement, and many thought that Munich had simply gained time. Preparations for national defence, including A.R.P., were pushed ahead more vigorously than ever. An A.R.P. Exhibition in Fulham Town Hall had been arranged for the period September 26-30, and thus coincided with the Munich crisis. This had the effect that some of the planned exhibits were not set up. People who did attend were particularly interested in the booklet 'Hints for Householders' describing the precautions to be taken against air raids. Preparations should be made to darken all rooms to comply with a general blackout. The attic and top floor should be cleared of all inflammable material as a precaution against incendiary bombs. A refuge room downstairs should be chosen. Upon hearing the air raid warning, people should proceed to this room taking their respirators. A wet blanket should be hung over the door to help keep out poison gas, windows should be tightly closed and the chimney blocked with crumpled newspaper. The emphasis was still on precautions against poison gas.

The influx of new recruits to Fulham's A.R.P. services had been welcome, but with the passing of the crisis there was a falling-off in public concern. To help stimulate interest, demonstrations were staged in seven different streets in Fulham to show methods of decontamination if poison gas were used. The main decontamination centre in the Borough was to be at the refuse destructor in Townmead Road. On December 8 a full-scale A.R.P. demonstration was held at Favart Road adjoining Eelbrook Common. A large crowd watched the rescue operations which would follow the dropping of a high explosive bomb, and the decontamination procedures to deal with poison gas. During the next few weeks cardboard cartons arrived for carrying gas masks, and these were distributed throughout the Borough. It was emphasized that, in the event of war, gas masks would need to be carried at all times. The Government decided that the shelter trenches dug on public open spaces should be put in good order and turfed over.

The Munich crisis had resulted in a widespread demand for better shelter provision. Just before Christmas 1938, the Government announced that a domestic steel shelter had been designed which gave good protection against bomb splinters, blast and debris. These shelters were to be supplied free to all lower income people in vulnerable areas. The shelter consisted of fourteen corrugated steel sheets to be sunk into the ground and bolted together, forming a corrugated steel hood. It would accommodate at least four people. The excavated soil was to be piled up around and over the shelter. The authorities made it plain that this shelter would not stand a direct hit, but would give good protection against a bomb falling nearby. Large-scale production of these so-called Anderson shelters was to begin immediately. The name Anderson arose from the fact that a distinguished civil servant, Sir John Anderson, had been brought into the Cabinet soon after the Munich crisis. He was given full responsibility for civil defence, with Government backing for all his work. In addition, a man named Anderson had taken a large part in designing the shelter.

A study of the bombing in Barcelona and Madrid had led to a feeling that high explosive bombs were a more immediate danger than poison gas. Ever since Munich there had been a growing demand for some form of deep shelters, and this was supported as a long-term policy by both the Parliamentary Labour and Liberal Parties. Fulham's A.R.P. Committee passed a resolution recommending that underground bomb-proof shelters should be provided. A Government enquiry later reported against any attempt to develop an extensive system of deep shelters because of the stupendous requirements of labour, materials and money that this would entail.

Another worry in the public mind which had come increasingly to the fore during 1938 was the question of evacuation from London and other large cities in the event of war. There was a general demand that the Government should accept responsibility for moving as many people as possible. By the end of the summer of 1938 this proposition had been accepted as Government policy. The country then had to be divided into three zones. Evacuation areas were the dangerous ones from which people would be moved. Inner London, including Fulham, was an evacuation area. Reception areas were those considered to be safe. Neutral areas were unlikely to have much bombing. Evacuees would be moved from evacuation areas to reception areas, but neutral areas would not be affected.

In January 1939 the Government announced the priority classes to be evacuated. They were (i) Schoolchildren in groups with their teachers; (ii) Younger children accompanied by their mothers; (iii) Expectant mothers; (iv) Adult blind people and cripples. At the time of the Munich crisis the London County Council had estimated, from enquiries, that 83% of parents with children at school wanted them evacuated. On this basis the L.C.C. had hurriedly drawn up plans to evacuate 637,000 schoolchildren. This total included the children in Fulham. Guided in part by the L.C.C. investigation, the Government decided to plan for the evacuation of eighty per cent of the eligible classes. For the whole country it meant arranging transport, food, accommodation and many other things for a total of four million people. This was going to be a huge undertaking. It was realized from the outset that billeting in private houses would be the only way to cope with the problem of accommodation.

Immediately after Munich the Government had carried out a careful review of all A.R.P. arrangements. It was generally agreed that the basic organization was sound, and did not need any substantial alteration. Earlier plans to divide the whole country into twelve Civil Defence Regions were finalized. A Commissioner was to be in charge of each Region, and would have general oversight of A.R.P. there. London was Region Number 5, and its headquarters were eventually established at the Geological Museum in South Kensington. The Region covered the entire Metropolitan Police District, and was sub-divided into Groups of local authorities. Fulham was part of Group Number 1, which included also Hammersmith, Chelsea, Kensington and Westminster.

In January 1939, following a Home Office Circular reviewing the numbers required for the various A.R.P. services, the situation in Fulham was re-examined. It was then calculated that a total of 3380 men and women would be needed in time of war. The total enrolled to date had reached 2369.

When Fulham's A.R.P. Committee met on February 7 notification was received from the Home Office concerning the public warnings to be used for air raids. The siren was confirmed for the general warning. If poison gas were used, the Wardens would go round the streets sounding hand rattles. When the gas was clear they would ring hand bells.

At its meeting on March 7 the A.R.P. Committee considered a Circular from the Home Office emphasizing the urgency of a final decision on the siting of Wardens Posts. Twenty-six locations were agreed for Fulham. Fourteen of the Posts were to be located in schools following upon the decision of the Government that schoolchildren would be evacuated and the schools closed in time of war. It was reported that an urgent house-to-house survey had been made in Fulham to ascertain where the new Anderson shelters should be erected. Many houses in the borough had small gardens, and in some streets there were outside lavatories. Great care would have to be taken in digging shelter positions to ensure that water and drainage pipes were not damaged.

In the middle of March there were further developments in Czechoslovakia. Following the Munich settlement the parts of the country not under German occupation had become disunited. On March 15 Hitler's troops moved into Prague, and Czechoslovakia became virtually a German protectorate. Public opinion in Britain was shocked because after Munich Hitler had stated that he had no further territorial claims in Europe. At the end of the month, Neville Chamberlain told the House of Commons that Britain and France would both support Poland if that country's independence should be threatened. A few days later the Government announced that the size of the Territorial Army was to be doubled. Local units immediately began placing full-page advertisements in the Fulham newspapers asking for recruits. These advertisements soon stopped because they were not necessary. The rush of volunteers was such that it was at first difficult to cope with them all.

In the Spanish Civil War, General Franco's troops had taken Barcelona in January whilst Madrid had surrendered at the end of March. The bombing of these cities had continued to be closely studied by the A.R.P. Department of the Home Office. One of the principal deductions was to confirm the long-established British estimate that one ton of bombs was likely to cause fifty casualties. One third of these would be fatal.

On March 28 Fulham's A.R.P. Committee received Government instructions that in the event of a 'national emergency' the Borough Council would need to appoint an A.R.P. Controller and an Emergency Committee. It was recommended that three Councillors would be sufficient for the Emergency Committee, but it was felt locally that six would be more satisfactory. Fulham's Town Clerk was to be A.R.P. Controller. It was reported that 1494 Anderson shelters had been delivered to houses in Fulham. As was expected there had been difficulty in fitting them into some of the small gardens, and subsequently sixty families had asked for the shelters to be removed.

A week later the Committee met again and was reassured to hear that work on the Wardens Posts was going well. Telephones had been installed in all the Posts so that the Wardens could make their reports on bomb damage to the Town Hall Control Centre. More recruits were still needed for the A.R.P. services, and it was decided to launch another recruiting campaign. The local boy scouts had agreed to help by distributing ten thousand leaflets throughout Fulham.

When Fulham's A.R.P. Committee met on May 2 they were informed that the latest expert advice was that one out of every hundred of the people in Fulham were likely to be killed in each air raid. Even though the population would be reduced by the evacuation of children and others, Fulham's Medical Officer considered that there could be one thousand dead in the Borough after each raid. If this dreadful situation should arise it was planned to open up long trenches two feet wide in Fulham Cemetery at Sheen.

The Medical Officer also reported that the projected use of Fulham Baths as a First Aid Post had been abandoned. It was realized from the beginning that this long narrow site would present difficulties. It was confirmed that the First Aid Posts would be at (i) Fulham Hospital in the old Guardians Offices; (ii) Western Hospital, Seagrave Road; (iii) West Kensington Central School; and (iv) Parsons Green Maternity Home. In London the L.C.C. was responsible for providing the Ambulance Service. This would need to be greatly expanded in wartime, and an establishment of seventeen thousand men and women had been decided upon. So far the L.C.C. had recruited slightly less than five thousand volunteers in response to public appeals.

The delivery of Anderson shelters in Fulham was being hurried along very effectively. A total of 5793 had been installed, although 164 had later been removed at the request of residents. The sight of these shiny steel shelters appearing throughout the Borough was making far more people realize the seriousness of the situation. It was obvious that the Government was very worried.

The Committee discussed a new Government handbook on incendiary bombs. This stated that an ordinary bomber could carry two thousand one-kilogram incendiaries, which would be released in batches of ten to twenty. Each batch would probably be contained in a light 'cage' designed to open as it neared the ground. The incendiaries would thus be concentrated in a small locality. The fire hazard was going to be considerable.

On 28 April 1939 the Government announced that military conscription was to be introduced. Young men aged twenty would have to register in June, and would be called up in July to be given six months military training. This was a modest effort compared with the countries of mainland Europe, but it was opposed by both the Labour and Liberal Parties in the House of Commons. Fulham Borough Council passed an emergency resolution opposing conscription. The Mayor of Fulham convened a special Town Meeting which also passed a resolution opposing conscription.

Late in May, local authorities received a Government instruction to give over-riding priority to civil defence matters for the next three months. All other municipal affairs were to be regarded as of less importance.

On June 13 the A.R.P. Committee considered a Circular from the Home Office urging further intensive efforts to complete the war-time establishment of A.R.P. volunteers during the next two months. Lectures and training exercises were in full swing locally, but Fulham still needed more volunteers. A request to the Home Office that uniforms should be provided had been rejected on the grounds of expense. The adjoining Borough of Chelsea had in fact provided uniforms for their Wardens, accepting that these would have to be paid for from the rates without any Government grant.

Notification was received from the London County Council that they were planning to have auxiliary fire stations at six places in Fulham. They were to be at: (i) The Rover Company premises, Seagrave Road; (ii) Harwood School, Britannia Road; (iii) The Gas Light and Coke Company, Malcolm House, Townmead Road; (iv) W. & M. Garage, 212 New Kings Road; (v) Fulham Central School, Finlay Street; (vi) Fulham County Secondary School, Munster Road.

On July 11 the A.R.P. Committee received a report on the further intensive efforts to recruit A.R.P. volunteers which had been urged by the Home Office. Five canvassers had been employed to make door-to-door visits in Fulham. In two weeks they had enrolled 276 Air Raid Wardens and fifty First Aid Volunteers. Metal discs had been ordered to mask traffic lights so that only a slit of light would show if a blackout were ordered. Large supplies of white paint and brushes were being stocked. Kerbs, trees bordering roads, and lamp-posts would all need marking with white paint if street lighting had to be extinguished. The erection of Anderson shelters in Fulham had gone well. Eight thousand had been delivered, although 465 had been removed at the request of residents. In fact the production of Anderson shelters had been on a remarkable scale. By the end of the month one million had been distributed throughout Britain.

The tense international situation was worsening. The German press and radio frequently carried reports of alleged Polish maltreatment of German nationals in Poland. In July the first of the young men required for the new militia were called up. The greatly expanded Territorial Army was at regular training, and night after night searchlights were being operated over London. In August naval reservists were mobilised. On August 23 the world heard the astonishing news that Germany and the Soviet Union had signed a pact of non-aggression. It was astonishing because Hitler had set out in the book 'Mein Kampf' his belief that Germany should expand to the east, into Russia and the Baltic States. Under the terms of the new treaty the Soviet Union had agreed to stay neutral if Germany were involved in war. Fulham's A.R.P. Committee met on the evening of the day the new pact was announced, and decided to order three thousand tarpaulin burial shrouds. In the light of all the information being supplied to the Committee this was a perfectly reasonable assessment of the likely requirement.

A steady stream of people began leaving London by road and rail. They were again heading mainly for the West Country and North Wales as had been the case at the time of the Munich crisis. There was no panic rush, but many of these evacuees were presumably going to accommodation provisionally reserved months before. From Southampton it was reported that five thousand people had left for the United States within forty-eight hours. Some of the people leaving London were from Fulham, mostly residents of the more affluent parts. Some big firms began preliminary moves of staff and records to hotels in towns such as Torquay.

Fulham's A.R.P. Committee was now superseded by the new Civil Defence Emergency Committee which met on Monday August 28. The Nazi-Soviet Pact had brought a feeling in Government circles that war was almost inevitable and there was a rush to complete preparations. Large quantities of sand or sandy soil were required for filling sandbags which were to be piled around key places. The sand from the children's sandpits in Bishops Park was taken, but this was a trifling amount compared with the requirement. South Park was to be the main local source of sand. There is a twenty feet thick bed of sand underlying Sands End, and in parts of South Park this was near the surface. Three mechanical excavators were brought in to dig out sand, and a total of eleven thousand cubic yards was eventually produced. Some of this went to other Boroughs. Government orders came to prepare for a general blackout. Fulham Council employees set to work with white paint marking the edges of kerbs, trees bordering streets, lamp-posts, etc., and painting many additional lines in the middle of roads. This work went on day and night.

Parliament had been recalled from the summer recess on August 24, and on the following day an Anglo-Polish treaty of mutual assistance was signed. Hitler then demanded that a Polish plenipotentiary should come to Berlin to negotiate a settlement. The Polish authorities refused. By this time German troops were massed on the Polish frontier.

At ten o'clock on the morning of Friday September 1 the B.B.C. broadcast the news that German troops had invaded Poland. Warsaw and some other Polish towns had already been bombed. The news spread rapidly and there was excitement everywhere. Buses and other vehicles passing along busy Fulham roads pulled in to the side and stopped so that their drivers could enquire what had happened. The news of the bombing was particularly alarming. It brought home to everybody the stark realization that London might indeed be bombed. At 11.07 a.m. the London County Council received orders from the Government to begin the evacuation of schoolchildren. Schoolteachers had been recalled from holiday earlier in the week, and some Fulham schools had been re-opened on Thursday to rehearse evacuation arrangements. Now the actual operation began. Children assembled at school bringing a change of clothes together with their gas masks. Each child was given a coloured shoulder strap identifying the school, while the teachers wore a white armlet bearing the school name. The classes then proceeded to the main line stations to be taken to their war-time homes. Fulham schools were evacuated to a variety of destinations, such as southwards to Gomshall, Guildford and Haslemere; or westwards to Windsor and High Wycombe. Lady Margaret School at Parsons Green was evacuated to Midhurst in Sussex. In the end it was found that fifty per cent of the children had been evacuated, many fewer than anticipated. When it came to the point, some parents could not face separation from their children.

There was a rush everywhere to get ready for the seemingly inevitable war. Fulham Hospital prepared to receive heavy casualties. Admissions were to be restricted to acute cases, and patients well on the way to recovery were sent home. Others were transferred out of London to safe places. Most of them went to Windsor to Old Windsor Hospital. Many emergency ambulances had been provided. As the Green Line buses completed their journeys that morning, they were stripped of their seats and fitted out as ambulances.

The Auxiliary Fire Service was mobilised, and reserve pumps were prepared for action. In London two thousand three hundred taxis were hired as towing vehicles, but were subsequently replaced by second-hand high powered cars. Eighteen hundred fire pumps were available immediately, compared with about 125 peace-time appliances. There were eight emergency fire boats on the Thames in addition to the three regular craft.

Radio announcements during Friday morning gave instructions for the mobilisation of all reservists for the armed forces and the Territorial Army. The trained Civil Defence volunteers in Fulham reported at the Town Hall. Those who were going to be on full-time duty had to be taken on to the payroll, and there was a rush of work setting up the necessary records. The Government had fixed the basic wage for men in the Civil Defence services at three pounds a week. This was regarded as a reasonable sum in those days. Women's wages were lower. Duty times were allocated so that Wardens Posts, First Aid Posts and the Town Hall Control Centre would have continuous basic cover in three shifts. The Control Centre was in the basement and had been strengthened with steel supports during the summer. It was from here that the deployment of local A.R.P. services would be controlled during air raids.

Sandbags were piled up round key points in Fulham such as the Wardens Posts. Broadcast appeals over the radio for volunteers to help fill sandbags met with a good response. It was estimated that approximately thirty thousand people went to South Park at one time or another to help fill these bags.

The Government ordered a complete blackout to operate at sunset on September 1. Dark material for curtains was quickly sold out in the shops, as were torches and batteries. Traffic lights and the lights of cars were masked to show only a slit of light. The use of headlamps was forbidden. Nobody dreamt that nearly six years were to pass before the lights could come on again.

During Saturday there were no developments apart from reports that Mussolini was proposing another conference rather like Munich. Nothing came of this. On Sunday morning September 3 at 11.15 a.m. Neville Chamberlain broadcast to the nation the news that Britain was once again at war with Germany. Thirteen minutes later the air raid sirens sounded their warning. People hurried to the shelters and waited apprehensively for the sound of approaching bombers. Church services were in progress and had to be terminated quickly. In some churches the congregations went down into the crypt. One Fulham vicar called upon his congregation to sing 'God Save the King' before dispersing. After nearly half-an-hour the all-clear sounded, ending what had apparently been a false alarm. As people emerged from their shelters they were surprised and impressed to see numerous tethered barrage balloons floating high over London. Balloon units had been established on many open spaces. In Fulham there were balloon units in the Hurlingham Club grounds, on the Eelbrook Common, in Bishops Park, and at Queensmill Road School which was renamed Queens Manor School in 1951. These barrage balloons, sixty-two feet long and twenty-five feet in diameter, had a hydrogen capacity of about nineteen thousand cubic feet. They were designed for a maximum flying altitude of five thousand feet. During the early hours of Monday morning the air raid sirens sounded again. Everybody got out of bed and went to the shelters, but once again it was a false alarm.

When Mr Chamberlain completed his Sunday morning broadcast he asked the nation to give close attention to the Government announcements that were to follow. These stated that all cinemas, theatres and other places of entertainment were to be closed immediately and that football matches and any events drawing large crowds were henceforth forbidden. Every citizen was enjoined to make sure that he had his name and address on his person at all times.

Many people who remembered the outbreak of war in 1914 remarked on the contrast in the national mood. The unconcealed emotional reaction of August 1914 was absent. At that time the country had not been engaged in a major war for a hundred years, and excited crowds gathered outside Buckingham Palace cheering enthusiastically. In September 1939 nobody had any delusions about war. The memories of the suffering and losses of 1914-18 were still vivid, and there was the new factor of likely large-scale bombing. Nevertheless there was a patient acceptance of the new war with Germany as a grim necessity. In Germany itself there was widespread surprise at the British declaration of war. The State control of news distribution in Germany had left people there in ignorance of world reaction to Hitler's successive coups.

CHAPTER THREE

TWILIGHT WAR TO REAL WAR

ON Monday September 4 the banks remained closed all day. The London Stock Exchange was closed for the whole week. In New York, 'frenzied buying' of company shares was reported because of the expectation of much larger profits resulting from the war. Many artistic and historic treasures were removed from London. The coronation chair went from Westminster Abbey, and the crown jewels were removed from the Tower of London. The National Gallery began taking its most important pictures to an underground slate quarry in North Wales. As had been the case at the time of the Munich crisis there was a big increase in the number of marriages. In fact the last few weeks of the summer of 1939 saw the highest marriage rate ever recorded in Britain.

During the next few days people went about their affairs expecting a German air offensive to start at any time. Everybody carried a gas mask. The Maternity Home at Parsons Green had been closed and had been transformed into a First Aid Post. The Babies Hospital in Broomhouse Road and the Day Nursery at Eridge House in Fulham Park Gardens were also closed. These closures were in line with Government policy that expectant mothers and children should be evacuated from London. In addition to the mortuary in Munster Road, temporary mortuaries had been established in Halford Road School and Langford Road School. All the schools had been closed for normal educational use. The teachers had gone to the evacuation areas with their classes.

There was no obvious German presence in Fulham in 1939 and no anti-German outbreaks as in 1914. Some enemy aliens were rounded up, and in London they were taken to Olympia before being moved to Butlins Holiday Camp at Clacton. Later the aliens were interned in the Isle of Man.

Everybody was to be given an identity card to be carried at all times. National Registration forms were issued to all households and in Fulham they were to be returned to Fulham Town Hall. National Registration night was Friday September 29. The small, folded manilla identity card was later posted to each applicant. The carrying of identity cards remained compulsory until 1952.

The Borough Council had acquired the responsibilities not only of Civil Defence, as the former Air Raid Precautions was being called, but of national registration and food control. Additional accommodation for the necessary staff was acquired at the Town Hall Mansions next to Walham Green (Fulham Broadway) Underground Station. The problem of conscientious objectors was dealt with by establishing a tribunal which met at the West London Magistrates Court in North End Road. The decisions of the tribunal were not announced publicly but were communicated in writing to the applicants.

Within a week of the outbreak of war, some local cinema owners approached the Mayor asking for his help in securing an easement of the Government restrictions on opening. People needed relaxation. The television service had closed down on September 1 but in any case very few people had television receivers. There was only one radio programme. The Mayor promised to make representations to the Home Office urging some relaxation of Government controls over places of entertainment.

There was a widespread feeling that the ban on public entertainments should be eased because there was no bombing. By September 14 all places of entertainment were allowed to open except between the hours of 10 p.m. and 8 a.m. In Central London the restriction was between 6 p.m. and 8 a.m. By the beginning of December there had been a general relaxation of restrictions except that 11 p.m. was fixed as the latest closing time. Dance halls were allowed later opening. There was concern in Fulham over the Chelsea Football Ground where the crowd in those days often numbered thirty thousand. Public air raid shelters in the vicinity could cope with only a fraction of this number.

The blackout was resulting in a sharp increase in the number of road accidents, and fatalities became double the peacetime norm. Pedestrians were particularly vulnerable and the Fulham newspapers carried reports of blackout fatalities nearly every week. London Transport produced posters and advertisements throughout the War, urging travellers to pause after leaving a bus or station so that their eyes would adjust to the darkness. Public pressure to ease the blackout restrictions led to debates in Parliament. Critics said that Paris allowed quite a lot of light, but the Government replied that Germany had even more stringent controls than Britain. The Air Marshals were adamant that a strick blackout was essential. Shortly before Christmas a slight easing of the restrictions was announced. Market stalls were allowed partial illumination, which was a great help in the North End Road market. Shops were also allowed a little lighting in their windows. A form of street lighting of very low intensity, requiring special fittings, was also authorized. This 'star-lighting', as it was called, could be left on during air raids.

Meanwhile the War was going on in what seemed to be a strange way. The R.A.F. was doing little but drop leaflets over Germany, and the army was not in action at all. Only at sea was there a struggle in progress, mainly in combatting German submarine attacks. The Royal Navy, weakened by reductions during the inter-war years, was strained to its limits. The complete lack of action on land, and the absence of the expected air raids, brought into use the expression 'phoney war'. This term appears to have originated in the United States. Neville Chamberlain called it the 'twilight war'.

Young men were required to register for national service on Saturday afternoons at their local Labour Exchange, the Wyfold Road Exchange being the centre for Fulham. Registration was arranged on an age basis, and those who registered could opt for any one of the three services. The actual call-up seemed slow as if there were no urgency.

Many of the mothers evacuated under the Government scheme soon returned home. If bombing had started immediately they might have stayed away, but as nothing happened they came pouring back. Only six weeks after the outbreak of war, a decision was made by the War Cabinet that mothers would be excluded from any future evacuation scheme. Time was to show that this decision was not irrevocable.

The continuing absence of air attack had important consequences. More and more parents brought their children home from the evacuation areas. By Christmas it was estimated that two thirds of the London evacuees had come back. There was growing public concern over the number of children roaming the streets all day without any schooling. The Fulham newspapers were carrying complaints of vandalism, including damage to air raid shelters and to homes left empty because their occupants had been evacuated. Eventually the Government announced on 1 November 1939 that schools in evacuation areas were to be re-opened for educational purposes as far as possible. The situation was difficult. The teachers were mostly in the reception areas with their schools, and some of the younger male teachers had already gone into the armed services. Empty school buildings had been quickly taken over for war purposes.

In Fulham a number of the Wardens Posts had been established in schools. West Kensington School housed various services. Halford Road and Langford Road Schools were mortuaries. The Auxiliary Fire Service had stations at Harwood School, Fulham Secondary School in Finlay Street, and Fulham County Secondary School in Munster Road. Large steel and canvas dams containing thousands of gallons of water had been set up in some school playgrounds to provide emergency water supplies for fire-fighting. To compound all these problems, large air raid shelters had not been provided at the schools because the children were evacuated.

Another problem which arose because of the so-called 'twilight war' was an attack on the Civil Defence Services by some sections of the press. Journalists were soon writing articles complaining of what they described as the 'colossal ramp' of air raid precautions. Large numbers of A.R.P. staff were said to be doing nothing, and the Air Raid Wardens came in for particular criticism. It would have been just as valid to say that large numbers of men in the army were 'doing nothing' but the point was not made. The majority of the A.R.P. force was composed of unpaid part-time volunteers, and the barrage of press criticism had a generally depressing effect on them. Eventually the Prime Minister had to point out forcefully that the German Air Force remained perfectly capable of delivering a heavy air attack at any time.

A general review of the Civil Defence Services was carried out because the Government was anxious to reduce expenditure wherever possible. Some personnel reductions were agreed in the Rescue and Ambulance Services. These were the responsibility of the London County Council. The First Aid Posts at West Kensington School and Parsons Green Maternity Home were closed, leaving just the two at Fulham Hospital and Western Hospital. The Fulham Civil Defence Committee carried out a review of women employees in Civil Defence. There were some 1,600,000 people registered nationally as unemployed at that time, and criticism was being expressed locally at the number of married women in the Civil Defence Services whose husbands were in employment. The categories affected seem to have been mainly among the canteen workers. Some of the married women were required to resign, to be replaced by other applicants judged to be in more urgent need of paid work. At the beginning of December it was reported that there were approximately one thousand paid members of the Civil Defence Services controlled by Fulham Borough Council. Uniforms had now been provided.

The Air Raid Wardens were being regarded more and more as key men in the organization to deal with air raids. It became necessary to lock shelters because of vandalism and the theft of light bulbs and other fittings. The Wardens had the keys, and it was their responsibility to open up shelters if the alarm were sounded. It was important to know who was likely to be in each house in case of bomb damage, and the Wardens had to keep in touch with people in their sectors. Babies 'helmets' for protection against poison gas were now becoming available in sufficient quantity to meet the demand. The term 'helmet' was being used instead of the original 'baby bag'. A small child's respirator suitable for children aged two to about four-and-a-half had been produced. To make it more acceptable to children it had a red rubber facepiece, blue container and bright eye-piece rims. This design became known as the Mickey Mouse mask. The Wardens had to help and advise on all matters concerning gas mask supply

In October it was agreed that Ackmar Road and Everington Street Schools should be re-opened for evening institutes and physical training. This was in line with the general move to restore recreational facilities. The closing of all the maternity and child welfare clinics at the outbreak of war was causing problems because so many mothers and child evacuees had returned. After a few weeks, emergency services were made available at the Eridge House Day Nursery in Fulham Park Gardens. In December the Parsons Green Maternity Home was partially re-opened.

The Government had recommended that local authorities should prepare plans for repairing war damaged buildings in co-operation with local builders. In Fulham a panel of local builders was formed comprising twenty-five local firms. It was intended that the repair of damaged buildings would be carried out by the Borough Council's Works Department supplemented by firms belonging to the panel. The Council's technical staff would organize the work.

Food ration books for the entire population had been printed before the outbreak of war. In November it was decided to distribute these by post, using the national registration forms as the basis for issue. The first foods rationed, from 8 January 1940, were bacon and ham (four ounces per person per week), butter (four ounces) and sugar (twelve ounces). It had been thought likely that bacon supplies from Denmark would be substantially reduced or stopped, but this proved not to be the case. As a result of the comparatively easy supply position, the weekly bacon ration was increased to eight ounces at the end of January. The price of butter had risen nearly twenty per cent since the outbreak of war, but margarine was unrationed and comparatively cheap. The demand for butter fell and it was possible to double the butter ration from 25 March 1940. Meat rationing began on March

11 with an allocation of 1s 10d worth of meat per week to every person over the age of six. A few weeks later it became possible to increase the value of the meat ration to 2s 2d. Offal was to be additional to the ration. Few people were familiar with the term offal, but it referred to such items as liver, kidneys and hearts. Meat was one of several basic foods which were subsidised by the Government in order to help control the rise in the cost of living which had followed the outbreak of war. The subsidies had been introduced the previous September in an emergency budget. This had also increased the basic rate of income tax from 5s 6d to 7s 6d in the pound to help pay for the war.

Petrol rationing had been introduced two weeks after the outbreak of war, but in those days very few Fulham people had cars. They were affected more by the fact that London Transport had to introduce some modification of the bus services because public transport petrol supplies had been reduced. There was a basic petrol ration for all cars, and it was not too difficult to obtain extra coupons for special circumstances.

The winter of 1939-40 was a hard one and temperatures over Christmas were below freezing. The difficulties of getting around in the blackout resulted in shopping in Fulham virtually stopping at darkness, although cinemas were doing good business in the evening. There were plenty of goods available in the shops although prices were going up. The official cost of living index rose quite sharply soon after the outbreak of war. By February 1940 the cost of food had risen by fourteen per cent, even though it was being generously subsidised. Clothing prices had risen by as much as twenty-five per cent.

More and more public air raid shelters were being constructed in a variety of situations. By the end of 1939 there were sufficient public shelters in Fulham to accommodate some eight thousand people. Some of the shelters were in the basements of large buildings, and others were surface shelters. Blocks of flats needed special provision. The Government and their advisers remained as certain as ever that heavy German air attacks could come at any time, but many of the general public were unconvinced. The anti-A.R.P. campaign in some of the newspapers had created doubt. An increasing number of Fulham people with Anderson shelters in their small back gardens were asking the Council to remove them. Some people said that they simply wanted the garden space. Others wished to grow vegetables. It would make no sense to go on constructing new public shelters and simultaneously to incur costs in removing and storing the steel Anderson shelters. By April 1940, one thousand applications had been received by Fulham Borough Council to remove Anderson shelters. It was decided to refer the matter to the Government for advice.

The London County Council was pressing ahead with plans to re-open some of the schools. In Fulham, St Dunstans Road, Munster Road and Queensmill Road Schools were to be brought back into use. The Borough Council's Civil Defence Committee was asked to arrange for the Wardens Posts at Harwood School and Fulham Secondary School in Finlay Street to be moved elsewhere. The Auxiliary Fire Service would have to move their station from the school in Finlay Street. On 9 April 1940 Fulham County Secondary School in Munster Road re-opened as the

West London Emergency Secondary School for Girls. Sloane School in Chelsea was opening as a Secondary School for Boys. These schools were to operate on a two-shift basis. There had to be a limitation of numbers in the schools at any one time because of the still-restricted air raid shelter accommodation. By the middle of the month the L.C.C. was able to announce that sufficient schools were being brought back into use to make compulsory school attendance possible. This would apply only to children aged between eight and fourteen, and was to be on a half-time basis.

The Government search for economies in Civil Defence continued. In March it was decided that the First Aid Posts at Fulham Hospital and Western Hospital should be placed on a care and maintenance basis. They could be activated at short notice if required. The trained volunteers who had been enrolled to operate the Posts would remain organized and ready for duties at short notice. The number of full-time Wardens was reduced to three hundred. Shelter Marshals were being enrolled to assist the Wardens in the control of air raid shelters.

During March and April the Ministry of Information and the local authorities organized a publicity campaign to encourage parents to register children of school age for evacuation should the need arise. Mothers and small children were not included. The press and radio were used extensively and millions of leaflets were distributed. The campaign was largely a failure. In Fulham only about one child in ten was registered and the situation was similar throughout London. Most people preferred to wait and see. They did not know what bombing would be like. They knew what evacuation was like, with families separated, and they wanted to avoid it if at all possible.

With the approach of spring the Bishops Park paddling pool was prepared for normal use. Sand was brought in to replace that taken for sandbags the previous September. In fact the stacks of sandbags around strategic places were being replaced by solid brick structures. The sandbags had been a temporary protection. Increasingly they were tending to split and spill, a process hastened by the habit of small boys of sticking their pen-knives into the sacks to watch the sand trickle out.

In general the War seemed to be only a background to life, having little effect on most people's everyday affairs. Few bothered to carry gas masks any more, and there was small public interest in the Civil Defence organization. Although many men were to be seen around in service uniform, the call-up remained quite leisurely. The only real war was still at sea. Enemy air attacks on coastal shipping were commonplace and mines were often laid in shipping lanes and harbour approaches. A new type of German mine, magnetically operated, had been introduced early in the War but had been successfully countered.

Food rationing remained slight and there was a wide variety of foodstuffs to be had. This was in no way comparable with the luxurious abundance of latter-day supermarkets, but at the time it seemed fully adequate. With the coming of milder weather and the light evenings, everybody was looking forward to some outdoor relaxation. The summer of 1940 looked like being an easy one.

Suddenly on April 9 the 'twilight war' came to an end. People switching on the B.B.C. early morning news at seven o'clock heard the startling report that German troops had invaded neutral Denmark and Norway. The small Danish army did not attempt resistance. The Norwegians fought and British troops were sent to help. It was to no avail. The British contingent was soon driven out. The King of Norway and his Government came to London to carry on the struggle from there. As a result of the Norwegian debacle Neville Chamberlain was forced to resign as Prime Minister. On May 10 a coalition Government was formed under Winston Churchill with Clement Attlee, the Labour Party leader, as Deputy Prime Minister. On the same day the German army invaded Holland and Belgium without warning.

Addressing the House of Commons in the afternoon Mr Churchill said: 'We are in the preliminary stages of one of the greatest battles in history' and continued, 'I have nothing to offer but blood, toil, tears and sweat'. The invading German armies advanced at astonishing speed and it became clear that the allied front was likely to collapse. There had been no successful invasion of England since 1066 which made it hard to visualize such a thing happening, but the threat was all too real.

Four nights after the invasion of Holland, the new War Minister Anthony Eden broadcast an appeal to the nation. A home defence force was to be formed immediately to be known as the Local Defence Volunteers. Their function would be to watch for landings of enemy airborne troops, man road blocks, patrol vulnerable points and so forth. The appeal was designed primarily for older men not liable for early call-up, and there was a huge response. Volunteers were asked to go to their local police stations to register, and soon after the broadcast a queue of men formed at Fulham Police Station in Heckfield Place. There was a similar response everywhere. Within twenty-four hours a quarter of a million men had applied to join the Local Defence Volunteers. The name was soon changed to Home Guard.

The Fulham Home Guard was the Third County of London (Fulham) Battalion and formed part of the South West London Sub-area. It was based at Fulham House near the river end of Fulham High Street. Many large establishments formed their own Home Guard Units. Fulham Power Station and the Gas Works at Sands End both formed Units because it was thought quite possible that German parachutists might be dropped to seize these important public services. There were also Home Guard Units at the Town Hall, the London Transport Building Department adjoining Parsons Green Station and the Drayton Paper Works by South Park. These Units were independent of the main Fulham Home Guard.

On May 15 the Dutch army capitulated, overwhelmed by sheer numbers, and Queen Wilhelmina and her Government came to London. Two days earlier, Fulham Borough Council had received a confidential communication from the Government asking that plans be prepared for the accommodation of war refugees from Holland and Belgium. The Civil Defence Emergency Committee decided on the Methodist Church Hall at 340 Fulham Road as a suitable dispersal centre. Part of St Thomas Church School in Rylston Road would be an additional centre if needed.

Another confidential Government notice reported that the Germans were now in a position to use a poison gas not guarded against in the existing civilian gas masks. An additional filter would have to be fitted, and it was suggested that the Wardens should do this work. More and more public air raid shelters were being constructed. Requests to remove Anderson shelters from Fulham back gardens stopped abruptly.

The Whitsun weekend had come, and the Government asked that the Monday Bank Holiday should be cancelled. The banks would open and all business be carried on normally. Some confusion followed. Official places opened all day but many private firms stayed closed. Some shops opened as did some of the stalls in the North End Road market. Most of them closed down at one o'clock since the day was obviously turning out to be more of a holiday than a working day.

In view of the gravity of the situation, King George VI called for a national day of prayer to be observed on Sunday May 26. On that day the King and Queen, accompanied by the Prime Minister and Queen Wilhelmina, attended service in Westminster Abbey. The churches in Fulham attracted large congregations as did churches everywhere.

The German army continued to drive forward at a remarkable rate and on May 27 King Leopold of the Belgians ordered the Belgian army to surrender. The Belgian Government came to London but the King stayed in Brussels. The allied front was breaking down, and the British Government decided that the only thing left to do was to evacuate the maximum number of men possible. 'Operation Dynamo', the evacuation from Dunkirk, began on May 27. No public announcement was made. During the next few days people in Fulham became aware that something big was happening. All day long, trains came pouring over the railway bridge from Clapham Junction into Fulham, and along Fulham's eastern boundary on their way to Willesden Junction. The trains were packed with soldiers who had been landed at the Channel ports. At Willesden the wounded were taken off. Some British wounded went to Fulham Hospital and some French wounded were taken to Western Hospital. The troop trains were then sent on their way dispersed to military depots all over Britain. The evacuation was a remarkable achievement, and a national day of thanksgiving was called for on the Sunday after its completion. There were far fewer people in Fulham's churches that day to give thanks than there had been for the earlier national day of prayer.

On the afternoon of June 10 Mussolini declared war on Britain. As the news spread it caused some excitement rather like the outbreak of war the previous year. This time the main public reaction was one of contempt. On June 18 General de Gaulle, the French Under Secretary for National Defence, flew to London. Four days later the French Armistice Commission sued for peace. Hitler then took control of a large part of mainland Europe, including the entire coast from Norway down to the Bay of Biscay. The British situation seemed desperate.

During the German advance the popular press had printed many startling reports of the work of Dutch fifth columnists and German parachutists. The term fifth columnist seems to have originated during the Spanish Civil War when a General said he had four columns advancing on Madrid and a fifth column of sympathisers inside the city who would rise to help him. In fact it was stated later that there were no Dutch fifth columnists. The newspapers also said that German parachutists had been dropped wearing various disguises, some even dressed as nuns. These stories seem to have been the product of journalistic imagination, but at the time people did not know that. Parachutists became a constant topic of conversation. A worried and alarmist atmosphere developed.

The police arranged for a constable to be on patrol at Putney Bridge at all times watching for saboteurs. The guards at the various A.R.P. depots in Fulham were provided with pick shafts and whistles. There was concern over this arrangement, and representations were made to the Civil Defence Emergency Committee that armed guards should be provided. The problem was that there were no armed guards available. The army was busy re-arming and re-organizing the men evacuated from France. The Home Guard in Fulham were drilling with such things as broomstick handles, an arrangement then common to the Home Guard everywhere. They were not armed until later in the summer when supplies of First World War rifles came from the United States. Security for the A.R.P. Report Centre in the basement of Fulham Town Hall was increased. Control 'gates' were installed and there was a strict identity check. Arrangements at the Reserve Report Centre at 706 Fulham Road were reviewed and some improvements made there.

All aliens serving in the Fulham A.R.P. Services were suspended. They had to be regarded with suspicion in case any of them were fifth columnists. Later it was agreed that some could be re-appointed but there was a generally hard attitude towards them. The aliens included a Russian, a Greek and several Czechs. An Englishman married to a German woman was also suspended. On May 27 the Government decided that all enemy aliens should be taken into custody. It was a hard decision because many were Germans of Jewish descent who had already been forced to flee their native country. They were anxious to help in the fight against Hitler. In fact, two months later Fulham Borough Council passed an urgent resolution on this subject. The resolution asked that 'tried and tested persons with a record of devoted service in the fight against Fascism' should be given an opportunity to serve this country. After the entry of Italy into the War on June 10 all Italians were rounded up. There were a few Italian nationals in Fulham mainly engaged in restaurant and hotel business. Most of the aliens were eventually interned in the Isle of Man, but in the course of time many were allowed back into normal life.

Government leaflets were soon distributed to every household advising people what to do in case of a German invasion. They were to 'stay put' so as not to block the roads. Rumours should not be spread. The Germans should not be given any help and bicycles and cars should be immobilised. In factories and shops managers should organize some system by which a sudden attack could be resisted. There was a general apprehension that German paratroops would be dropped in large numbers.

Orders were issued that all place-names should be removed, wherever possible, so that invading Germans could not verify the location. Presumably this was intended to apply mainly in rural areas, but the name Fulham was carefully obliterated on public buildings in the Borough. In country areas thousands of signposts and milestones were removed and carted off into store. In mid-June a total ban was imposed on the ringing of church bells for all normal purposes. They were to be rung only as a warning if enemy parachutists landed nearby. The bells of All Saints, Fulham became silent. On level fields to the south of London concrete obstacles were positioned at intervals to prevent the landing of German gliders. Late in June, at the request of the War Office, the Fulham newspapers published silhouettes of a German troop-carrying aircraft to help people identify the enemy. In July the military asked Fulham's Civil Defence Emergency Committee to set up concrete defence posts on the approaches to Putney Bridge and the new Wandsworth Bridge. Defence posts were also required at the junction of Lillie Road and Seagrave Road. The Auxiliary Fire Service began training fire-fighting parties all over Fulham. Groups of people got together and were shown how to use a stirrup pump to extinguish an incendiary bomb. The Groups were then issued with a pump so that they formed a street fire-fighting party.

On July 18 the German army staged a great victory parade in Berlin. The war was over as far as the Germans could see. On the following day Hitler addressed the Reichstag appealing 'once more to reason and common sense in Great Britain as much as elsewhere . . . I can see no reason why this war must go on.' In fact Winston Churchill had already rejected any idea of giving in, an attitude wholeheartedly supported by the nation. Intensive preparations continued in readiness for an invasion attempt which seemed certain to be made. As a precaution the Bank of England gold reserves were taken to Canada in a British warship. A new budget increased the standard rate of income tax to 8s 6d in the pound.

In 1939 at the outbreak of war many London schoolchildren had been evacuated to the coastal areas of South-East England and East Anglia. At that time these were safe localities but the German occupation of France and Belgium had completely changed the danger map of Britain. Many Fulham children were in Surrey but do not seem in general to have gone further south. Lady Margaret School at Parsons Green had been evacuated to Midhurst in Sussex. This was only fifteen miles from the coast but the decision was made to 'stay put'. Children within ten miles of the likely invasion coast were quickly transferred elsewhere. In June, as the French battle front disintegrated, the Government put into operation a new evacuation scheme for London children. Approximately eighty thousand of them left the London County Council area, including many from Fulham. The capital seemed curiously empty as people waited for the expected German onslaught. In July London Transport was advertising special buses on some Sundays to take Fulham people to visit their children evacuated to Stoke Poges and Slough.

Before an invasion of England could be attempted the Germans had to achieve command of the air. During May and June, German aircraft either singly or in small formations penetrated over Britain with growing frequency. Over two thousand high explosive bombs were reported as having been dropped as well as approximately five thousand incendiaries. By the end of June the frequent air raid warnings were causing serious losses of production in factories. Work stopped and employees went to the air raid shelters until the 'all clear' sounded. The Government then decided on a change of policy. Work was to continue after the sounding of a public air raid warning until an attack seemed imminent in the vicinity.

Soon after the Dunkirk evacuation there had been a marked acceleration in the call-up of young men who had registered for military service. This affected the A.R.P. services as their younger members were taken from them. Local authorities such as Fulham, who felt sure their areas would soon be under air attack, were concerned by this loss of personnel. The Government considered the matter, but decided there could be no deferment of call-up even for key members of A.R.P. services.

Early in August Fulham Borough Council was informed by the Government that refugees from Gibraltar were going to be accommodated in North End House, North End Road. It was thought quite possible that General Franco might take action over Gibraltar, possibly assisted by the Germans. Some 10,500 inhabitants of the colony were brought out as a precaution.

Meanwhile the Germans had put in hand an intensive programme of works to prepare the captured airfields in France, Belgium and Holland for operations against Britain. By the third week in July these works were largely completed, as also was the replenishment of the German Air Force units. They had suffered serious losses during the fighting in Europe, but had been re-grouped and were ready to take the offensive. The enemy had available a large bomber force, and fighter squadrons which were of much the same quality as the British fighters but numerically superior. With their new bases only one hundred miles from London, all the German bombers could come with full bomb loads escorted by fighters. No theoretical 'worst case' studied by British defence chiefs before the War had been as bad as this.

The German onslaught began on August 13 with the main purpose of destroying R.A.F. Fighter Command. Hard-fought daily air battles continued relentlessly until early September, and the main R.A.F. airfields in South-East England were all severely damaged. On the evening of August 15 enemy bombers managed to penetrate even into the suburbs of London and bombed Croydon Airport which had been taken over by the R.A.F. The cumulative effect of these attacks on airfields had been to place the entire R.A.F. Fighter control system under great strain. Then in early September Hitler ordered a change of tactics.

Towards four o'clock on the afternoon of September 7 British radar detected large formations of enemy aircraft building up over the Pas de Calais. Before long, massed formations of bombers and their fighter escorts were advancing along the south of the Thames estuary towards London. It was estimated that there were some 350 bombers and 600 fighters. R.A.F. Control ordered up most of their fighter squadrons in South-East England and positioned them to protect the already battered airfields. But this time the Germans were not going for the airfields. London was the new target. The British fighter squadrons were badly placed to intercept and the German bombers struck hard sustaining only small losses.

CHAPTER FOUR

THE BLITZ: SEPTEMBER-DECEMBER 1940

SATURDAY September 7 was a fine sunny day and many Fulham people had been out enjoying the weather. Late in the afternoon the air-raid sirens sounded, and before long anti-aircraft fire and the thud of bombs could be heard away to the east. After about an hour the 'all-clear' came, but as darkness fell the whole sky was glowing bright pink. The streets were illuminated by what was obviously a tremendous fire. Clouds of smoke were drifting overhead and there was an acrid smell of burning. People gathered in the streets in small groups quietly discussing events and wondering apprehensively what the night would bring. No announcement had been made in B.B.C. news bulletins, but everybody in London soon knew what had happened. Large numbers of German bombers had attacked the docks area and the East End and huge fires were burning. All the Fulham fire pumps had gone to help fight the blaze, and fire appliances from brigades to the south of London had been seen streaming across Putney Bridge on their way to the docks. In fact, before the night was out, fire appliances were brought in to help from as far away as Birmingham and Bristol. It was a spectacular start to what was to become known as 'the Blitz', an abbreviation of the German word blitzkrieg or lightning war. In the evening the sirens sounded again and the bombers came back. This time they concentrated on spreading the area of fire by bombing around the perimeter of the blaze. Some bombs were also dropped in Westminster and Kensington, but there were still none in Fulham.

The first bombs in Fulham came in the early hours of Monday September 9. At 0300 a high explosive bomb fell at 132 St Dunstans Road. Four other high explosive bombs fell in that area of Fulham soon afterwards, presumably aimed at Hammersmith Railway Station. The most spectacular damage was a direct hit on one block of Fulham hospital. This incident has been recorded by a painting held in the Fulham local history collection. Fortunately the hospital block had been cleared in readiness for the expected air raid victims and there were no casualties. The blast from this bomb blew out all the front windows in the new Keir Hardie House opposite the Hospital. An oil bomb fell at the junction of Rannoch Road and Nella Road but failed to ignite. These oil bombs were similar in outward appearance to the standard high explosive bombs, but their casings were made only of thin pressed sheet steel. They were filled with a heavy inflammable oil mixture and had a central burster charge of three pounds of explosive. If an oil bomb failed to ignite, as was often the case, it burst open and left an extensive oily mess. Soon after the bombing in the north of Fulham, there came a successful attack on Fulham Power Station. At

0350 there was a direct hit on the turbine house, causing serious damage to the plant. Several men were killed. Electricity was supplied from Fulham to much of London, so the reduction in output caused problems. A second bomb at the Power Station, dropped at the same time, failed to explode and was removed by the army on the following day. Early on the Monday evening, two bombs fell at Bishops Park. One landed in the area of the bandstand, and the other fell in the river close to the embankment.

Late that night more bombs fell in Fulham, some in the northern part of the Borough and others within range of Parsons Green. An oil bomb exploded at the junction of New Kings Road and Munster Road. Seven incendiaries were reported. There was a tragic occurence at the Munster Road end of St. Dionis Road where a bomb had fallen. A.R.P. personnel were at work rescuing injured people when at midnight a delayed action bomb suddenly exploded. Ten A.R.P. workers were killed.

The bombing then settled into a pattern throughout the whole of September, with German aircraft attacking targets in Fulham nearly every night. As soon as it was dark the sirens sounded. Soon afterwards the throbbing of aircraft engines could be heard overhead. The bombers had one engine running faster than the other so that the alternating noise confused sound detectors. It was dangerous to be out after dark, and railway stations were prime bombing targets. Offices, shops and factories all had to close early so that everybody could reach home in daylight.

Within forty-eight hours of the mass bombing of the docks on September 7, anti-aircraft guns had been moved into London from all over Britain. The number of guns in the capital was doubled. In spite of this increase Londoners were generally dissatisfied with the anti-aircraft barrage. It seemed to them that the bombers were flying around with impunity. On September 10 the commanders of all the gun positions in London were called to the Signals Drill Hall in Brompton Road, Kensington, for an urgent meeting. There it was decided that every gun was to fire every possible round that night. There would be no searchlights operating and no R.A.F. fighter aircraft over London. The resulting intense firing of anti-aircraft shells delighted Londoners, and cheers went up in the crowded air raid shelters. There were some people, however, who thought the constant bangs were more bombs falling. These people emerged at daylight expecting to find widespread destruction. In fact the guns had no means of firing accurately at bombers. The Commander of Anti-Aircraft Command had to report in his official despatch that the firing was 'largely wild and uncontrolled'.

That night fifteen high explosive bombs fell in Fulham together with three that failed to explode. There seemed to be some concentration towards Barons Court Station and also the industrial complex along Townmead Road by the river.

The night of September 11/12 passed with only four high explosive bombs in Fulham concentrated in the central area, but six anti-aircraft shells came down. These landed in the central part of Fulham, possibly having been fired from the same gun. Unexploded anti-aircraft shells were a problem. Gun barrels became worn through heavy use, and then failed to rotate shells sufficiently to 'arm' their fuses. The production of gun barrels was not sufficient to meet the demand for replacements. Another difficulty which developed was that the clockwork fuses in the anti-aircraft shells were not reliable and the shells failed to explode in the air. Before the War these fuses had been imported from Switzerland, a source of supply which was now shut off. There were not enough skilled workers in the United Kingdom to meet the new demand, although the position did gradually improve. The anti-aircraft shells which came down often fell harmlessly. On other occasions they exploded, sometimes causing fatalities. Fulham Borough Council was asked to arrange for some of their employees to undertake the digging up and collecting of unexploded shells, a task which was said not to be inherently dangerous. This arrangement left the army Bomb Disposal Sections free to concentrate on unexploded bombs.

The night of Friday September 13 brought tragedy into Fulham. Of the eleven high explosive bombs recorded, one hit a large surface air raid shelter in Bucklers Alley. It was the largest surface air raid shelter in Fulham, designed to accommodate twelve hundred people in a number of separate compartments. The shelter was built on a site later occupied by the Brunswick Boys Club. There were thirty-eight deaths. On the same night the Fulham Telephone Exchange in Lillie Road was hit and put out of commission.

The weekend of September 13/15 brought only a little activity over Fulham until the early hours of Sunday. Then a German bomber attempting to attack the Sands End Gas Works was brought down. Pieces of the aircraft were scattered over a wide area of Fulham, suggesting that it blew up in the air. The body of the pilot was found in the street near the Borough Council's Munster Road Depot. In his possession was an aerial photograph of the extensive Gas Works with notes on it in red ink indicating key points to aim at, such as gas holders and coking plant. It is not known what happened to the rest of the crew. They may have baled out.

Only a week had passed since the first mass attack on the East End of London, but already many Fulham people were experiencing the effects of bombing. A house did not necessarily have to be hit. A bomb nearby could bring down ceilings, filling rooms with white plaster dust. Alternatively, soot might tumble down chimneys coating everything in black dust. Slates came off roofs. Windows and doors were blown in by blast. Shattered windows became a great problem especially with the onset of colder weather. There was not enough glass to carry out the necessary repairs, and many windows had to be boarded up. Some people had glued criss-crossed brown paper over their windows to hold the glass together. Its effectiveness varied. After a house had been hit by a bomb there was a sickly-sweet smell of mortar dust. In the morning there might be no water or gas because bombs had damaged the mains. People got into the habit of filling up kettles and other containers with water every evening.

Many surface shelters built in the streets had white concrete roofs, and some people were worried that bomber pilots might see these roofs and aim at the shelters. To allay public fears, Fulham Council workmen began colouring the roofs. A powerful searchlight on Eelbrook Common caused considerable concern. It was said to be the second brightest in London, and tended to illuminate the tall chimneys of the Power Station. There was a widespread public belief, which in fact was well founded, that bombs were sometimes aimed at searchlights. The commander of the Eelbrook Common searchlight battery was asked to meet the Mayor to discuss the matter, and the searchlight was eventually moved away in December.

During the night of September 15/16 fourteen high explosive bombs fell in Fulham. One hit a coal conveyor belt at Fulham Power Station, and two fell in the Sands End Gas Works. The following night five bombs were reported but one at 17 Lysia Street failed to explode. It was removed by the army two days later. September 18/19 brought six high explosive bombs and reports of twenty-six incendiaries.

The next few nights saw a similar pattern of bombing with some eight or ten bombs each night, but on September 25/26 there was a particularly heavy attack. Fulham had fifty-two high explosive bombs that night and about the same number of incendiaries. The bombing was spread all over the Borough, although there was some concentration in the northern part. These latter bombs may have been aimed at the railway line linking West Kensington, Barons Court and Hammersmith Stations.

The next few nights brought only minor activity, but October 1/2 was unusual. Nine high explosive bombs fell in Fulham that night, and every one failed to explode. Seven came down in the grounds of the Hurlingham Club and two in South Park. In due course all the bombs were either detonated or removed. The Hurlingham Club grounds were the location of anti-aircraft batteries, searchlights and barrage balloons. This was obviously a good position to help protect the important riverside industrial complex nearby, and these defences attracted the attention of the German pilots.

Unexploded bombs were proving to be a problem. In February 1940, a decision had been made to establish Bomb Disposal Sections as part of the responsibilities of the Royal Engineers, and at the end of June their numbers were substantially increased. When the intensive bombing of London began it was found that approximately one in ten of the bombs dropped failed to explode. Most of these unexploded bombs contained a delayed action device using a clockwork mechanism. The clockwork often stopped, either because of a weak spring or a minute fault in the milling. A slight jolt could easily re-start the mechanism so that handling delayed-action bombs was a hazardous enterprise. Casualties among the Bomb Disposal Sections in the early months were heavy but the work had to go on. Unexploded bombs resulted in roads being closed, factories shut down and undamaged houses left empty. In many cases these bombs caused more disruption than the ones that went off. Towards the end of the summer, an apparatus known as a 'steam-sterilizer' became generally available. A hole was cut in the case of the U.X.B. and the main explosive filling was emulsified by an injection of steam and drained away. The remainder of the operation was then comparatively straightforward.

As the days grew shorter the raids grew longer, and sometimes the 'all clear' came so late that it was not worth going back to bed. The 'all clear' siren was now being sounded for only one minute instead of two. People were tiring but the absenteeism rate from work caused by sickness actually fell. There was a dogged determination to keep going. People became talkative, friendly and companionable in a way not usual in peacetime. Some of the larger shops were displaying a poster, which had been widely distributed, bearing a portrait of Queen Victoria. This carried a quotation from one of her letters, written at the time of the South African War – 'We are not interested in the possibilities of defeat. They do not exist.'

In order to make the maximum use of daylight, the advancing of clocks by one hour for Summer Time had been introduced earlier in the year than usual, at the end of February 1940. A decision was later made to leave Summer Time in operation right through the winter until the following year. Clocks were advanced a second hour in May 1941, making them two hours fast on G.M.T. They were brought back one hour in August 1941. In the subsequent years of the War, Double Summer Time was introduced in late spring and ended at dates which varied between July and September. Thus Greenwich Mean Time was not used for everyday purposes during the remainder of the War.

Before the War nobody had anticipated a situation in which bombing would go on all night. With winter coming on, there was concern over the problem of providing warmth in shelters because many people spent the whole night in them. An official shelter census made in London at the beginning of November showed that twenty-seven per cent of the estimated population spent the night in household shelters, predominantly Andersons, whilst nine per cent went to public shelters. In addition the Underground Stations accommmodated four per cent of London's population.

None of Fulham's railway stations provided public shelters below ground, although in the early months of the bombing some people made a habit of crowding into the pedestrian tunnel linking Willowbank with Bishops Park. At the beginning of October the Government announced that bunks were to be provided for all public shelters. Many people were already taking bedding into the shelters and spreading it out as best they could. Some wanted to leave their bedding, but Fulham's War Emergency Committee decided that bedding must be removed each morning. The Medical Officer was anxious that all shelters should be cleaned and disinfected daily.

The early part of October saw a limited amount of bombing. It was mostly with the standard 250kg high explosive bomb, but during the night of October 11/12 an oil bomb fell in the Gas Works at Sands End. This damaged some of the working plant. The only other incident recorded that night was a high explosive bomb on the air raid shelters at the William Parnell municipal flats near the Gas Works. Four people were killed.

Bombing increased sharply for the next few nights. Twenty high explosive bombs were recorded for October 13/14 together with two unexploded ones. They fell mainly in the southern part of Fulham. On the following night sixteen high explosive bombs fell in Fulham, two of them hitting favourite targets. One was the Club House in the Hurlingham grounds and the other the Gas Works at Sands End. Forty incendiaries were also reported.

On the night of October 16 there was a full moon, 'bombers moon' as it was called. Before radar was developed as an effective means of locating aircraft after nightfall, a clear moonlit night was ideal for bombing. An estimated four hundred

German bombers attacked London that night, making it the heaviest assault since the bombing of the docks on September 7. Just over one thousand high explosive bombs were dropped on London, but only nineteen of these fell in Fulham. Three of them failed to explode, two of these falling harmlessly in Bishops Park. Twenty-one incendiary bombs were reported in Fulham, but this was a tiny proportion of the estimated seventy thousand incendiaries dropped on London. Clearly the Germans had come to the conclusion that the incendiary bomb was a very effective weapon. One of Fulham's churches was destroyed. It was St. Augustine's at the junction of Lillie Road and Moylan Road. London's railway stations were a particular target. Five main line termini were put out of action, and a number of other stations were damaged.

On the following night thirteen high explosive bombs fell in Fulham, and the Borough also had its first parachute mine. At the outbreak of war the Germans had introduced magnetic mines, dropped from aircraft by parachute for use against shipping. Counter-measures to deal with these new mines were successful, but some of them came down in built-up areas well away from the sea. These had probably been dropped in error. The magnetic mine incorporated a self-destruction appliance which operated if the mine came down on land. Cylindrical in shape, and eight feet long by two and a quarter feet in diameter, the magnetic mine had a powerful blast effect. Graphic newspaper reports of the damage caused in built-up areas by these accidental 'drops' made the German Air Force realize the potential of the magnetic mine for use against large towns. A proportion of parachute mines, slightly modified for their new role, was then allocated to be dropped in bombing raids. The Royal Navy was responsible for 'rendering safe' any unexploded mine. The Navy also 'swept' the Thames regularly up as far as Hammersmith in case any mines fell into the river. The mine which came down in Fulham during the night of October 16/17 did explode. It fell in the Jervis Road/Mulgrave Road area and the blast caused widespread damage. Mulgrave Road is located at the eastern end of Normand Park, but Jervis Road was cleared away after the War to help form the Park.

London's public transport system was under great strain. The persistent hammering of railway stations and railway tracks by the bombers, together with the destruction of many buses, was slowing down the busy life of the Metropolis. The Ministry of War Transport asked for buses to be sent from provincial towns all over Britain to help. They came from as far afield as Inverness in the north and Plymouth to the west. In Fulham the number eleven bus route was soon augmented by some of these buses. Among the first to be seen were buses from Halifax in Yorkshire, followed shortly afterwards by some from Huddersfield and Leeds. Buses from Scottish towns were also seen passing through Fulham. All these extra buses were useful, and eventually nearly five hundred operated in London. Later, when the bombing of provincial places became heavy, the buses were returned to their own towns.

It is sometimes said that war brings out the best in some people and the worst in others. A problem which developed during the bombing was looting from damaged houses. Men from various civil defence services would converge at a newly bombed house, and thieves who had managed to acquire steel helmets could mingle with them. Recognition was difficult in the darkness, and the thieves managed to get into the bombed premises. On the other hand it was often the case that very valuable items were recovered by Civil Defence workers and brought into safe custody.

Before the outbreak of War, both the B.B.C. and the German radio organization were broadcasting in each other's languages to put their points of view to listeners overseas. These broadcasts continued after the War had begun so that for the first time in history people could hear the enemy speaking to them in their own homes. One broadcaster from Germany eventually became a household name. He was William Joyce, born in the United States of an Irish father. Joyce settled in England and became a member of the British Union of Fascists. He went to Germany in 1939, and soon began broadcasting to Britain. He became well-known to the British public as 'Lord Haw-Haw'. Many people listened to him, and he was often credited with statements that he never uttered. Claims that Lord Haw-Haw had announced that certain places were to be bombed became widespread during the War. There were pub rumours in Fulham from time to time that 'Lord Haw-Haw' had announced a forthcoming raid on the Borough. Alternatively, after some of the bad nights, rumour had it that 'Haw-Haw' had forecast the attacks. These reports appear to have been largely imaginative. After the War, William Joyce was brought to London and charged with high treason. He was found guilty and hanged.

During the latter part of October there was some bombing in Fulham but it was comparatively light. Unfortunately an anti-aircraft shell which had failed to explode in the sky, crashed down on Fulham Palace Road School during the night of October 19/20 killing six people. The school was in use as a rest centre for those bombed out of their homes. People who had been made homeless were accommodated temporarily in one of the rest centres in the Borough until arrangements could be made to billet them in an empty flat. The rest centres and the numbers they were sheltering at this time were: Fulham Palace Road School (later Melcombe) sheltering 268 people, Lillie Road School (later Sir John Lillie) with 201 people, All Saints School 112 people, and St James Church Hall 50 people. Chelsea and Fulham Railway Station in Wandon Road, close to the Chelsea boundary, was hit and caught fire on the night of October 21/22. The damage was extensive and the station was not used again.

First-aid repairs to houses to make them weatherproof would later enable some of the bombed-out to return home. People whose homes were damaged beyond repair, and were unable to make their own arrangements, were able to stay in billets. There were plenty of empty flats in Fulham at that time because many families had gone away to safer areas. A report made to Fulham's War Emergency Committee on October 19 showed that, up to that time, five hundred people had been billeted after losing their homes. It is interesting that many people were refusing to be settled in the West Kensington area where there were numerous empty flats. That part of Fulham seemed to be getting an unduly large share of the bombs falling in the Borough. St Pauls School, situated in Hammersmith but close to the Fulham boundary, had been taken over by the army. It was thought that the

School was attracting the bombers. The railway was another target.

On October 26 the Borough Engineer made a report summarising the bomb damage situation in Fulham. A total of 350 properties had been wrecked, or were in such a state that they would need to be demolished. Eight hundred others were badly damaged and required extensive repairs. First-aid repairs were being carried out to large numbers of other houses. Sixty-one roads in the Borough were at that time closed to traffic because of bomb craters, unexploded bombs or adjoining dangerous buildings. The river wall by Bishops Park had been badly affected, forty-five feet of it having been demolished. Furniture from damaged houses was being removed and stored either in the Market Hall, which adjoined the Town Hall, or in Kelvedon Hall in Kelvedon Road. One of the most valuable services to bombed-out people was to recover their personal effects. This gave them hope of eventually re-establishing a home. Another useful service concerned telegrams. After heavy air raids on London, large numbers of telegrams were received from anxious people in other parts of the country addressed to relatives. If the telegrams could not be delivered for any reason, it was agreed that they could be held at the local Town Hall.

The two war-time mortuaries in Halford and Langford Road Schools were lit by gas in those days, but bombing in late October had damaged gas mains causing a complete temporary breakdown of gas supplies thereabouts. Electric lighting had been installed as an emergency measure.

A further report to Fulham's War Emergency Committee on November 2 showed a reduction in the number of people living in emergency shelters. This reduction resulted from the lull in bombing. There were sixty-six homeless people in Fulham Palace Road School and 140 in Lillie Road School. Nearly one thousand 'bombed-out' people had been found 'permanent' living accommodation.

During November the lull over Fulham ended. On the night of November 6/7 eighteen high explosive bombs were dropped, including one which failed to explode. After this there was a fair amount of bombing on most nights. The record for the night of November 10/11 is remarkable in recording a fall of twenty-five bombs in Fulham, of which no fewer than nineteen failed to explode. These UXBs (unexploded bombs) were all safely removed during the next few days.

There was no bombing in Fulham on the night of November 12/13, but in adjoining Chelsea there was a direct hit on the then new Underground Station buildings at Sloane Square. It was 10 p.m. and a train was just leaving the station. Forty-two people were killed. A call for help was made to neighbouring areas, and Fulham sent two Rescue Parties.

November 14/15 was a peaceful night in London with no bombs falling, but the early morning B.B.C. news bulletins quoted German radio reports of the mass bombing of Coventry. No official British comments were available until later, but then they confirmed the German claims. The centre of the city had been devastated. The news was chilling, and people wondered if this type of concentrated mass attack would become more common.

On the following night there was a full moon, and the whole of London came under heavy attack. Fulham had eighteen high explosive bombs, one of which brought tragic consequences. This was a 500kg bomb, twice the size of the standard German bomb, and it hit numbers 80, 82 and 84 Greyhound Road. The bomb penetrated to a basement air raid shelter under number 82 and killed twenty people. Another bomb hit an Anderson shelter in the garden of 21 Epple Road, killing one man. These Anderson shelters were proving very satisfactory, standing up well to bombs falling within a short distance of them. They could not survive a direct hit. Many people who had originally refused an Anderson shelter were now clamouring for one, and there was a waiting list. On the same night as the Greyhound Road tragedy the grounds of the Hurlingham Club, with their concentration of guns, searchlights and barrage balloons, again attracted the bombers. Four bombs fell in the grounds and a fifth hit the East Block of the adjoining Rivermead Court, penetrating four floors.

On November 16 the Borough Engineer reported that 'first aid' repairs had by then been carried out to no less than 6,900 properties in Fulham. This work was designed simply to make homes weatherproof by repairing roofs, doors and windows. The Borough Council's direct labour force, together with the Fulham Panel of Builders, had been responsible for the repairs. Forty-four roads in Fulham were closed to traffic as a result of the bombing. Many lorries were required to cart away debris. Some were being hired from contractors, and others were lent by the army.

The number of people living in the Emergency Centres had been reduced to 148. The first delivery of the standard Government bunks for public air raid shelters was expected shortly. It was estimated that their installation would reduce the capacity of the shelters by fifty per cent, but many more public surface shelters were under construction in Fulham or planned.

On the night of November 16/17 another parachute mine floated down towards Fulham, but was exploded high up in the air over the Thames some little way north of Fulham Football Ground. Presumably it had been hit by anti-aircraft fire. Some windows were broken by the blast but there was no serious damage. Ten high explosive bombs fell in Fulham that night, mostly in the southern part of the Borough. Two of the bombs failed to explode. An Anderson shelter at 14 Burlington Place received a direct hit but there were no casualties. The usual occupants of the shelter had decided not to leave the warm house that night because they had a baby with them. A considerable number of incendiaries fell in the Fulham Road/Fulham Palace Road area, starting some small fires. The roof of Munster Park Methodist Church at the corner of Fulham Road and Chesilton Road was destroyed by fire. The following night was relatively quiet with eight high explosive bombs in various parts of Fulham. There was now a lull in the bombing so far as Fulham was concerned, although every night at dusk people waited apprehensively for the sound of the sirens. A novelist writing of those times referred to the daytime as 'a curious holiday from fear'.

On November 21 Councillor da Palma died suddenly. He was highly regarded in Fulham and had been Mayor during 1939-40. Councillor de Palma had taken a leading role in getting A.R.P. preparations started before the War in the face of much local apathy and active opposition. A portrait of him, wearing the steel helmet which he had as Chief Warden, hangs in the council chamber of the Old Town Hall at Fulham. Alderman Gentry succeeded him as Chief Warden.

On the night of November 29/30 there were five high explosive bombs round about the Eelbrook Common area, together with one oil bomb which fell opposite 2/4 Crondace Road. There was to be only one more bomb in Fulham before Christmas. It fell on the night of December 3/4 at the St Dunstans Road entrance to Fulham Hospital, but the damage was not serious. Following the destruction of one entire block on the night in September when Fulham was first bombed, the hospital had been hit on two further occasions. The damage both times had been so bad that all the patients had been evacuated until essential repairs were carried out.

CHAPTER FIVE

THE BLITZ: DECEMBER 1940-MAY 1941

SOME complaints had been made in Fulham that the small amount of street lighting permitted was in fact too bright. Investigation showed that the worries usually arose where buildings near street lights were painted white. People were afraid that this would attract bombing. The Rescue parties and other A.R.P. workers were emphatic that a minimum of lighting was essential for them to operate in the blackout, and the lighting was left as it was. Problems arose later when some people tampered with lights near their homes to make them inoperative. Eventually the War Emergency Committee had to state that prosecutions would be initiated if the lights were not left alone.

Early in December the Borough Council's War Emergency Committee received representations from the Fulham Trades Council urging the construction of bomb-proof shelters sufficient for all residents and workers in Fulham. The Committee felt that the idea was impracticable. Their reasons were similar to those which emerged from the Government enquiry on deep shelters in 1938.

In a report made on December 7 the Borough Engineer listed the areas of Fulham which had suffered most damage from bombing. They were: (i) Lillie Road towards North End Road; (ii) Charleville Road; (iii) Horder Road; (iv) Delvino Road; (v) Purcell Crescent; (vi) Basuto Road. The demolition and clearance of wrecked properties in Fulham was likely to take many months, and there was an acute shortage of transport and cranes.

The most accurate estimate of the size of Fulham's population at that time could be obtained from the number of ration books issued in the Borough. These totalled 88,000 compared with the 1938 estimated population of 137,000. During November the London County Council again made a considerable effort to persuade parents whose children were with them to consider evacuation to a safe area. The campaign had little success. A check in the Borough Council's housing estates showed that two thirds of the children were away in safe areas. The parents of the remaining one third had no wish to let their children go. These proportions are likely to have been similar for the whole borough.

By December, public air raid shelters had been provided in Fulham sufficient to accommodate 55,000 people. This was considered enough. The new government bunks for the shelters were beginning to arrive and 3,300 had already been delivered. The standard of lighting and sanitation was being improved. Enquiries were being made concerning the provision of refreshments. A camaraderie had developed in most of the shelters with the same people going to the same places

—47—

night after night. They were drawn together by the common danger and many new friendships were made. People living on their own did not want to remain isolated during an air raid. The number of full-time Wardens was being restored from 250 to 300, and more part-time Shelter Marshals had been enrolled to help with general supervision. The lull in the bombing had resulted in only eighty-four people needing to be accommodated in the emergency centres.

December remained quiet in Fulham, and just before Christmas the War Emergency Committee received a report on the situation to date. Since the bombing began in September, a total of 395 high explosive bombs had been reported in Fulham. Most of them were of 250 kg in weight. Fifty of the bombs had failed to explode, and had been dealt with by the military. Forty-two anti-aircraft shells had come down in Fulham, of which six had exploded on impact. Borough Council workmen had dealt with most of the others. First-aid repairs had been completed to 8823 houses. At one time and another, 115 roads had been blocked by craters or debris. The clearance of rubble remained a big problem, and the Government had decided that men of the Pioneer Corps would be made available to help with this work.

The Fulham Battalion of the Home Guard had settled down to a routine, as had the various independent units in the Borough. The consignments of First World War rifles brought over from the United States in July had ended the days of drilling with broomsticks. The rifles were coated with grease which took a great deal of cleaning off, but once ready they were excellent weapons. The main training area of the Fulham Home Guard at this time was Number 1 Polo Ground of the Hurlingham Club. After the War this became the Hurlingham Park athletics centre. People living nearby complained of the noise of explosives while the training was in progress, but they had to accept the position. 'There's a war on' was becoming a standard reply in such situations. The Headquarters of the Fulham Battalion remained at Fulham House in the High Street. Later a Company Headquarters was established in North End Road School. This school was demolished after the War. It was situated just south of the North End Road/Lillie Road junction. Guards were mounted regularly at Putney Bridge, the then new Wandsworth Bridge, Fulham Town Hall, St Pauls School in Hammersmith Road and the railway junction at West Brompton Station. On Sundays a control was operated on Wandsworth Bridge by inserting steel posts into holes drilled in the road. This forced the traffic to proceed slowly along a zig-zag route, thus providing the Home Guard with an exercise in checking enemy forces advancing into Fulham. The various special Home Guard units in Fulham continued to operate separately, but the one at the Power Station was disbanded in February 1941.

Shopping at Christmas was difficult because of the blackout and the resulting restriction of shop hours. Most goods were still obtainable, but the over-running of Europe by the German armed forces had necessitated a marked extension of food rationing.

Sugar, butter and bacon had been rationed since January. On June 10 the bacon ration had to be halved to four ounces weeky. This was a direct result of the German invasion of Denmark which had cut off an important source of supply. Meat had been rationed since March, but the maintenance of the ration proved difficult. In peacetime there had been large imports of frozen meat from New Zealand, Australia and South America. Once the Germans had the whole of the French coast under their control, additional U-boat bases were soon established. From July 1940 onwards, the losses of British shipping from submarine attack increased substantially. It was not until the summer of 1941 that this onslaught was mastered, and sinkings greatly reduced. Just before Christmas, 1940 the meat ration was cut from 2s 2d worth to 1s 10d. Reduced imports necessitated a further reduction on January 6 to 1s 6d, but for several weeks customers often had to accept a proportion of corned beef in their ration. By mid-summer of 1941 the meat ration was down to 1s 2d. It remained at this low level for the rest of the War. Fortunately, fish was usually available and this became an important element in the nation's wartime diet.

Margarine and cooking fats had to be rationed from July, following the cessation of all imports from mainland Europe. Tea rationing was also introduced in July. German bombers had established bases in Sicily and closed the passage of the Mediterranean to British shipping. As a result, tea being brought from India had to be brought round South Africa, and the longer journey reduced the amount which could be imported.

Milk was a special case. In July 1940 a national milk scheme had been introduced. This provided that every child under five, and all expectant and nursing mothers, should have a pint of milk daily at just under half price. Poorer families would get their milk free. The scheme was an immediate success, so much so that although milk production increased it later became necessary to ration milk supplies to non-priority customers.

There were shortages of cheese and fish. Fresh fruit, much of which had been imported before the War, was becoming just a memory. Many minor items of 'luxury' foods, such as tinned fruit, were virtually unobtainable. Fortunately, bread was never rationed. Potatoes were usually available in good quantities, especially later in the War when production was substantially increased. The Ministry of Food often had newspaper advertisements urging people to eat more potatoes.

On the night of 27/28 December 1940, German bombers made a massive incendiary attack on the City of London. This attack was timed to take place at the lowest ebb-tide, which made it difficult for the fire-boats to operate from the river. Water mains were broken early on by large high explosive bombs. Before long there were major conflagrations in the square mile, and these left a ruined void in the vicinity of St Pauls Cathedral. There were no incidents in Fulham that night, except that a wire basket of incendiaries, which had failed to open, fell at Stamford Bridge Stadium. It caused little damage and seems likely to have been a 'stray' from the main attack on the City. Incendiary bombs were packed in containers with air-burst fuses which were timed to explode and scatter the incendiaries during descent.

During the first three months of 1941 there was very little air raid damage in Fulham, a total of only seven high explosive bombs falling in the Borough during those weeks. The Germans had redirected the main weight of their bombing away from London to provincial towns and especially to the ports. The limited amount of bombing in London was mainly on the east and south-east of the capital. It was realized that a renewed German onslaught directed at London could come at any time. The records of the Fulham Registration District had been moved from the Town Hall to a disused lift shaft deep under Piccadilly Circus. They remained there for the duration of the War.

Compulsion for fire prevention duties had been under discussion for some months, and the experience of the great incendiary attack on the City of London brought matters to a head. On 15 January 1941 new Regulations agreed by Parliament provided that anybody within certain age limits could be compelled to perform part-time civil defence duties. Local authorities were required to make adequate arrangements for dealing with fires in prescribed business and industrial districts, where there was virtually no residential population. The Wardens were recruiting volunteers to form more fire-fighting parties, and by the end of January two thousand people had been enrolled in Fulham. They were trained in parties of three to extinguish incendiary bombs with a stirrup pump, and each group was then issued with a pump. Sandbags partly filled with sand were placed by the street lamp standards throughout Fulham to be available for extinguishing incendiary bombs. The sandbags were subsequently replaced by sandbins. Sandmats, flat bags made of sacking and filled with sand, were produced later and distributed around the Borough. They could be tossed on to a burning incendiary and proved quite effective. Later in the War, when the Germans used explosive incendiaries, the sandmats were withdrawn.

Early in March, Fulham Borough Council's War Emergency Committee received a report on the various premises in use at that time for civil defence purposes in which arrangements had to be made for fire prevention.

Places in use for storing furniture from bombed houses, or earmarked for that purpose, were: the Market Hall by the Town Hall, Bethel Chapel and Ebenezer Chapel in the North End Road, Queens Club and Fulham Cross Garage.

Rescue Party depots were established at West Kensington Central School (later Mary Boon School), Cobbs Hall and the Public Baths at Walham Green opposite St Johns Church.

There were First Aid Posts at Parsons Green Maternity Hospital, West Kensington Central School, 129 Fulham Palace Road adjoining Fulham Hospital, and in a small part of the Western Hospital in Seagrave Road.

The Wardens Posts were mostly in schools, but some were in blocks of flats such as the then new Burne Jones House, West Kensington Court and Rivermead Court. Other locations were in places such as St Etheldreda's Church Hall and Fulham Constitutional Club.

Queensmill Road School housed an R.A.F. Balloon Unit. Auxiliary Fire Service detachments were based in Ackmar Road and Finlay Street Schools.

Preliminary arrangements for more fire-watching in the Borough were proceeding satisfactorily. The Wardens had been making a house-to-house canvas, and eight thousand people had been enrolled as potential members of fire-watching parties.

The position regarding public air raid shelters was reviewed at the beginning of

January. The two largest surface shelters in Fulham were the one in Bucklers Alley which had been repaired and could again accommodate twelve hundred people, and another in Fulham Park Gardens which held 750 people. The trench shelters constructed in the Borough's open spaces at the time of the Munich crisis were in good order. They had been well used during the bombing. The Eelbrook Common shelter held 1876, the one at Lillie Road Recreation Ground 1866 and the South Park shelter 1402. Mains water was to be laid on at all the large shelters. A canteen service provided by a private contractor had been authorized to visit them regularly. The worst part of the winter was still to come, and experience of the long night air raids had shown the importance of making shelter life reasonably comfortable.

At its meeting on 24 January 1941 the War Emergency Committee in Fulham received a strictly confidential circular from the Government emphasizing that the possibility of poison gas attack remained very real. The Committee was asked to review immediately all arrangements for dealing with gas. The general presentation of the circular suggests that the Government had cause to suspect that the enemy might be contemplating the use of gas. It was known that large stocks of poison gas were available in Germany, but fortunately British preparations to deal with this threat had been very thorough. Perhaps that is why it was never used.

By the end of March the lull in the bombing had resulted in the rest centres being empty. A total of 1846 bombed-out people had been billetted with private families. Another 332 were living in privately-owned flats and houses which had been requisitioned, and 457 had been rehoused in flats owned by Fulham Borough Council. A recent check of the Council's housing estates had shown that fifty-five per cent of the children were away in evacuation areas.

Large quantities of building material salvaged from war-damaged properties had been accumulated at Heckfield Place where slum properties in 'the Avenues' area had been cleared away just before the War. In March 1941 there were in store 230,000 roughly cleaned bricks, 1500 slates, 1800 tiles and 50 baths. Good lengths of timber had been accumulated totalling approximately 25,500 ft. run. Dumps of firewood from bombed houses had been established at the Lillie Road Recreation Ground and South Park. The public were invited to help themselves to this firewood, and were making good use of the facility.

The general position regarding food supplies changed little during the early weeks of 1941. Oranges were available briefly during January, and greengrocers were asked to make an allocation of one to each customer. Apart from this there was hardly any fresh fruit until home grown supplies became available in the early summer.

Wheat supplies were causing concern at the Ministry of Food. In March the disquieting fact came to light that flour consumption had increased by ten per cent, possibly owing to the reduction in the meat ration. Most wheat was imported, and German submarine and surface vessels were sinking large numbers of allied vessels. It was suggested that only wheatmeal bread should be made available instead of white bread, because a given quantity of wheat would make approximately 12½% more wheatmeal than white bread. Eventually it was decided not to stop the making of white bread, but to organise a national advertising campaign to persuade people to eat wheatmeal bread. This campaign went on for months but achieved little success. By the end of 1941 consumption of wheatmeal bread was only four per cent of the total eaten, compared with three per cent when the campaign began.

In December 1940 President Roosevelt had put forward the idea of 'lend-lease', an arrangement by which goods from the United States could be supplied to Britain without payment. On 11 March 1941 this became the law of the United States. It was a development of vital importance to the United Kingdom, already short of foreign exchange to pay for imported goods. Food could be supplied under lend-lease as well as war materials.

The spring offensive by the German air force continued the pre-Christmas pattern. It was directed mainly at provincial towns and in particular at ports. Then on the night of April 16/17 there came another heavy attack on London. The centre and the south of the metropolis bore the brunt of the raid, and Fulham was little affected. But the bombers were bringing an increasing number of parachute mines and two of these came down in Fulham. One was at Duckhams Wharf in Stevenage Road and the other at Comleys Wharf, Townmead Road. Neither of the mines exploded, and they were subsequently rendered harmless by naval personnel and removed. Fulham was lucky to get off so lightly, because that night's attack proved to be the worst on London so far. At one stage all Southern Railway stations were closed, several stretches of the Underground Railway system could not operate, and road transport was badly disorganised. Gas supplies were severely interrupted because of broken mains.

On the night of May 10/11 the bombers again attacked London on a scale similar to that of three weeks earlier. Once again Fulham was fortunate because the onslaught was directed mainly at the capital's centre, and the eastern and south-eastern districts. Only seven high explosive bombs fell in Fulham, all in the Hurlingham area. Of these bombs two fell in the grounds of the Parsons Green Cricket Club, a third on the playground in South Park and a fourth on the foreshore off Hurlingham. Westminster suffered badly that night with 193 high explosive bombs, two parachute mines and hundreds of incendiaries. Many important buildings were destroyed or damaged. The Chamber of the House of Commons was burnt out. Westminster Abbey and numerous other national shrines were damaged. The Mayor of Westminster was killed whilst visiting public air-raid shelters. Under an arrangement known as 'mutual assistance' Fulham sent Rescue Parties and Stretcher Parties to help. Subsequently a letter was received from the Westminster City Council expressing 'warmest appreciation' of the help given. Mutual assistance was in fact becoming a regular feature of civil defence operations. If Fulham was having a quiet night, help could be sent elsewhere if needed, usually to Westminster or Chelsea.

CHAPTER SIX

HOLDING ON: MAY 1941-DECEMBER 1941

FOR the next few weeks people waited apprehensively at dusk for the familiar sound of the sirens but nothing much happened in London. There was some limited bombing in the provinces, but the Germans were already moving aircraft in readiness for an invasion of Russia. This began on 22 June 1941. The German advance was rapid and nearly all responsible military opinion held that the Russian armies would soon be destroyed. Winston Churchill warned the nation that Germany retained a bombing force in the west 'quite capable of making very heavy attacks'. The Civil Defence Services had to be retained in a high state of readiness.

The Wardens Service had proved of key importance during the bombing and the Commissioner responsible for civil defence in the London Region commented: 'We do not think that anyone realized before the battle began the extent to which the Wardens Service was pivotal.' By the spring of 1941 the number of full-time Wardens in Fulham had reached the designated total of three hundred. There were also five hundred unpaid part-time Wardens. The name Shelter Marshal was discontinued and they became part of the force of part-time Wardens.

By the end of the winter of 1940-41 bunks were being supplied for the Anderson shelters as well as for public shelters. But once people had grown accustomed to night bombing, many preferred to stay in their houses rather than go into a cold Anderson shelter in the garden. Some who had taken refuge under their staircases or under a strong table, had been rescued unhurt after a bomb had hit their home. The Government therefore decided to introduce a new type of shelter suitable for use on the ground floor of a house. This shelter had a rectangular steel framework six feet six inches long, four feet wide and two feet nine inches high. The top was made of steel plate and experiments showed that it would sustain the collapse of two higher floors. Two adults and two children could sleep in the shelter. It was known as a 'Morrison' shelter after the Minister of Home Security Herbert Morrison. These new shelters became available from the end of March 1941 but were issued sparingly.

A considerable effort was being made by the Government to stimulate national savings. Wages had gone up sharply but the supply of goods in the shops was falling. It was important to draw money out of circulation to help check the rise in inflation. Each borough had its own special week allocated for a savings drive, and in Fulham War Weapons Week was to be May 17-24. The slogan chosen by the local Savings Committee was 'Help to Buy Fifteen Bombers'. These were said to cost £20,000 each. A special exhibition of war relics was staged in the premises formerly occupied by Timothy Davies shop at 2/6 Fulham Broadway. A large drapers store had occupied this building for many years. The exhibits included an unexploded German bomb which had fallen in Bishops Park. A new tank stood at Fulham Broadway for public inspection, having been first driven around Fulham at what was said to have been an alarmingly high speed. Many buildings were decorated with flags and bunting, together with posters urging people to save. A parade of Civil Defence personnel, with bands, marched through Fulham on the closing Saturday of War Weapons Week. The final total of savings raised locally that week was £200,000.

How best to meet the enormous costs of war was a continuing problem. In his April budget the Chancellor of the Exchequer had raised the standard rate of income tax to ten shillings in the pound and lowered the exemption rate. Part of the money collected was to be repaid after the War as 'post-war credits'. It was the Government's intention to stabilize the cost-of-living index at twenty-five per cent above the pre-war level. Subsidies on food were to be increased as necessary.

At its meeting on May 23 the War Emergency Committee received another report on war damage in Fulham. To date, the number of houses which had been demolished or were in process of being demolished totalled 494. A further 1185 had been badly damaged but could be completely repaired in time at a reasonable cost in relation to their value. Minor damage, such as slates off roofs or broken windows, had affected 10,157 houses. The number of people who had been 'dishoused' at one time or another was approximately 10,000. Fulham's population stood at 86,000, a reduction of 2000 compared with six months earlier. A survey had shown that there were 3170 habitable dwellings vacant, a substantial proportion of these being in the West Kensington area. Some changes were being made in the arrangements for storing furniture from bomb-damaged houses. The use of Ebenezer Chapel, Bethel Chapel and Fulham Cross Garage was to be discontinued. The hard tennis courts at Queens Club were to be added to the area already in use there for storage purposes.

There was a continuing strong demand for allotments. Some additional land had been made available in South Park and at the Parsons Green Cricket Club, but more was needed. Eventually arrangements were made with the Ranelagh Club at Barnes to use some of their extensive grounds, and 396 plots were provided there for Fulham gardeners.

In order to make the best use of food waste, pig bins had been placed at restaurants and housing estates in the Borough. This innovation had been successful, and subsequently pig bins were placed in streets all round Fulham. A substantial amount of food waste was collected by this arrangement and sold to farmers. In 1942 Westminster City Council established a special plant in Pimlico for the sterilization and concentration of kitchen waste. Adjoining boroughs were able to deliver their waste to the plant, and Fulham joined in the scheme.

The special arrangements for supplying milk to priority classes had led to a rise in consumption, and it became evident that supplies would not be sufficient to meet the demand. At Easter 1941 retailers' supplies of milk were cut by one seventh and deliveries to non-priority customers had to be reduced. Shortly afterwards the weekly cheese ration was reduced to only one ounce for a time because of the shortage of milk, but in June the ration went back to two ounces. After that the ration rose steadily thanks to lend-lease supplies from the United States. By the summer of 1942 the cheese ration had reached eight ounces, and it remained at that level until early in 1943.

Before the War approximately half the eggs sold in Britain had been imported, principally from Denmark and Holland. These imported supplies were no longer available and it proved very difficult to control the commercial production and distribution of eggs. By June 1941 the allocation of eggs had to be set at one per person each week. It was not possible to fix a guaranteed ration because supplies could not be guaranteed. In September, owing to a seasonal falling-off in supplies, the allocation of eggs was reduced to one a fortnight. Fortunately the Department of Scientific and Industrial Research had been asked in 1940 to develop a method of producing dried egg powder suitable for domestic use. The research had been successful, and arrangements were made for the large-scale production of dried egg in the United States. The manufacturing arrangements took time but deliveries began in June 1942.

By the summer of 1941 there were shortages of some goods in the shops. In order to conserve both shipping space and foreign currency, imports of many materials were being restricted. Clothes rationing was introduced on May 31, and to start with a spare page of margarine coupons in the normal ration book was used for clothing. This arrangement caused difficulties, because in some cases shop assistants had inadvertently taken the spare page. In August, when the validity of the ration books expired, a clothes rationing card was issued in Post Offices in exchange for the front cover of the old ration book. Unfortunately many people had scrapped their old ration books and they arrived at the Food Office in Fulham Town Hall in some numbers to see what could be done. Eventually their problems were sorted out. Difficulties continued until 1943 when a special clothing book was incorporated with the new food ration books. In the event, clothes rationing remained in operation until March 1949.

Shortage of labour was becoming a serious problem, with all men aged between twenty and forty liable for military service unless in a reserved occupation. It was necessary to rely far more on women, and a new Employment Order required women aged twenty and twenty-one to register for war work. In Fulham these young women registered at the Wyfold Road Labour Exchange in June 1941 and stated what employment they were in. They could subsequently be directed into war work, although many were granted exemption because of domestic circumstances. As the War went on the ages between which women could be directed for war work were steadily increased until they covered the range eighteen to fifty. Women were quickly accepted as a necessary part of the industrial scene.

In the middle of June it was reported that the George Medal had been awarded to two men, and the British Empire Medal to three others, employed in the Gas Works at Sands End. The awards had been for gallantry the previous autumn when bombing had started fires among the gas holders. The men had checked the outbreak by closing inlet valves to the holders and various other measures. A large coke dump had caught fire and burnt for some weeks.

With the coming of summer, and the long lull in the bombing, people were feeling relaxed. Less than half of the general public were making a practice of carrying their gas masks. At the end of June arrangements were made for some Wardens to release cylinders of a harmless smoke near Walham Green (now Fulham Broadway) Underground Station at a busy period. The intention was to bring home to people the fact that poison gas bombs might be used by the enemy at any time. The effort was received with good-humoured banter from the passing crowd.

The growing scale of the fire raids had caused the Government to reconsider the organization of the fire services. The general policy on civil defence was to rely on the local authorities to organize and operate the various services, but it was felt that many local authorities were not large enough to cope with widespread fires started by numerous incendiary bombs. From the beginning of August 1941 a National Fire Service began to operate. England and Wales were divided into thirty-three Fire Areas. London was large enough to stand on its own, and originally formed one of the areas. Later, in May 1942, the London fire services were divided into five areas subsequently reduced to four. The final organization left Fulham, Hammersmith, Acton and North Kensington grouped together as Fire Force Area Number 34. A valuable innovation was the establishment of a system of observation posts to detect fires at an early stage. The hose-drying tower at the Fire Station in Fulham Road was the most important local observation post. A look-out could report the direction and approximate location of any fire so that appliances were quickly on their way to deal with it.

Another change in August 1941 was that people performing fire prevention duties were to be known as Fire Guards. Members of street fire-fighting parties had worn an armlet with the letters S.F.P. New armlets were supplied bearing the name Fire Guard. Growing shortages of manpower nationally had caused the Government to issue an Order requiring compulsory registration for the part-time Fire Guards. Men aged 36-60 were the first required to register. At its meeting on September 12 the War Emergency Committee was told that Fulham had 12,610 potential Fire Guards. There were numerous claims for exemption as provided for in the Government Order and these took some time to deal with.

In July new ration books were issued to be collected from the Food Office at Fulham Town Hall. The ration of basic goods remained unchanged, but many minor foods were 'in short supply', an expression becoming familiar in war-time Britain. Queues for such foods were commonplace, and shoppers often joined a queue without first bothering to find out what it was for. The supply of milk was an increasing problem. The 'priority' classes continued to take up their full allocations. Dairy farmers could not produce sufficient milk to meet the remaining demand because imports of feeding stuffs for cattle had been greatly reduced. Local dairymen had to ration their customers according to the availability of supplies, and with the coming of winter the position became increasingly difficult. Some dried milk and evaporated milk were issued to dairymen in lieu of fresh milk to ease the problem, but there was a good deal of grumbling from the general public. The theft of bottles of milk from doorsteps increased. The Ministry of Food issued newspaper advertisements explaining the difficulties and emphasizing that 'Children Come First'.

At the beginning of December special welfare foods were made available for young children and expectant or nursing mothers. These foods were cod liver oil and fruit juice. The cod liver oil came from Iceland. The fruit juice at first was blackcurrent purée, soon to be replaced by concentrated orange juice from the United States. These foods were supplied at cheap rates or free. There was disappointment that only half the mothers applied for them in spite of a Ministry of Food advertising campaign. There was a particularly small demand for cod liver oil. Welfare foods remained available throughout the War but consumption always remained low.

In December 1941 a new and very useful addition to food rationing was introduced. This was the points system based on a scheme already operating in Germany. The object was to ensure a fair sharing-out of any foods which were available only in very limited quantities. A new points ration book was to be issued in which the coupons each represented so many points. Foods available under the scheme were valued at a given number of points, which could be varied according to the availability of supplies. Three groups of food were used to inaugurate the scheme. They were canned meat, canned fish and canned beans. The new points ration books were to be issued on presentation of the old ration books. In Fulham, to obviate the need for everybody to journey to the Town Hall, points ration books were also distributed at the public libraries. The points scheme was an immediate popular success. In January 1942 dried fruits, rice, sago, tapioca and pulses were made available on points; in February canned fruit, tomatoes and peas and in April breakfast cereals and condensed milk. The quantities of these foods available on points was always very limited, but they provided a little welcome variety to the restricted war-time diet.

Fulham people had enjoyed a summer of peace in 1941, free from bombing, but there came tragedy on Wednesday October 22 when a British fighter aircraft crashed in Gowan Avenue. It was just before six o'clock in the evening. There was no air raid in progress, and witnesses spoke of the sound of an explosion from the aircraft before it came down. The body of the pilot was lying in the road opposite 93 Gowan Avenue. Parts of the aircraft were scattered far and wide, one wing landing in Fulham Cemetery.

By the middle of 1941, making the most effective use of manpower had become a key factor in the war effort. When Winston Churchill formed his Coalition Government in 1940 he had appointed Ernest Bevin to be Minister of Labour. Bevin was not a Member of Parliament. He was Chairman of the Trades Union Council, and was to be responsible for the maximum mobilisation of Britain's manpower during the war years. If the full demands of the armed services and civil defence were to be met over the next twelve months, said the Minister of Labour in August 1941, this would involve the withdrawal from industry of approximately one million men. In addition some two-and-a-quarter million men and women would have to change their occupations. The Minister went on to say that changes on such a scale would be possible only if the nation was prepared to give up 'not only amenities but many things that have been looked upon as almost necessities.' In December Fulham's Civil Defence Committee, which had replaced the War Emergency Committee, was informed that the training of Wardens was to include instruction in first aid. The separate First Aid Posts were to be reduced in number, and the Wardens would help with first aid. This was an early indication of changes being made to economize on manpower in the Civil Defence Services. The minimum age for most Wardens was to be raised from thirty to thirty-five to release men for the armed services.

In November the army placed a new searchlight on Eelbrook Common. This soon brought complaints from local people, and the Civil Defence Committee decided to ask that the searchlight be removed. In a letter to the local Commandant the Committee referred to the 'enormous damage to neighbouring property . . . last year' when the previous searchlight was operating. A few days later the reply came that the new searchlight was 'temporary for trial purposes'. However, just before Christmas a letter from the Civil Defence Regional Commissioner for London arrived intimating that the searchlight would have to remain. In fact during 1941 an improved radar for use with searchlights in detecting aircraft had gone into production. It may well be that the new searchlight was fitted with this radar which was code-named 'Elsie'.

During 1941 the British army was fighting in North Africa, R.A.F. bombers were often attacking places in Germany and the Royal Navy was still principally engaged in combatting the U-boats. The biggest land operations were in Russia where the German army was driving relentlessly forward. Most military experts still expected that Russia would eventually be forced to capitulate, thereby immensely strengthening the German position in Europe.

Some people saw grounds for optimism. In July 1941, Dr Edith Summerskill, who had been M.P. for Fulham West since 1935, referred to the War when opening an art exhibition in Fulham. She said 'the War should be over this time next year. In my optimism I sometimes think I might cut that period in half and say the War will be over in six months'. By contrast, in September another well-known Fulham personality put a sharply contrasting point of view. Mr J.W. Banfield, a Fulham Councillor and M.P. for Wednesbury, gave his opinion that 'this will be a long and bitter war'.

In December a succession of events underlined the gloomier forecast. On Sunday afternoon December 7 a large force of carrier-borne Japanese aircraft made a surprise attack on the American fleet lying at a base on an island in the Pacific. It was Pearl Harbour, a place few people in Britain had heard of before. The United States declared war on Japan the following day as also did the United Kingdom. Three days later Germany and Italy declared war on the United States. The conflict had become world-wide. A few days later Japanese carrier-borne aircraft achieved another success when they sank the new British battleship Prince of Wales together with the battle-cruiser Repulse. It was a worrying Christmas.

Late in 1941 the Government had decided that iron railings everywhere, unless necessary for public safety or of artistic value, were to be cut down and used for scrap. The Ministry of Works was responsible for this operation and employed contractors to do the work. There were some complaints of poor workmanship, perhaps inevitable in view of the general shortage of labour. Opinions varied as to the aesthetic results of removing railings. When the iron railings round Parsons Green had been removed, many people commented favourably on the resulting appearance of a pleasant village green. Doubt was expressed later as to whether the removal of railings was ever necessary. Some local authorities had difficulty in finding scrap merchants prepared to collect their dumps of railings.

CHAPTER SEVEN

WORLD WAR: JANUARY 1942-DECEMBER 1942

IN the pre-war planning for A.R.P. careful attention had been given to the necessity for ample water supplies to fight fires. One proposition had been to establish large storage tanks at selected places, capable of holding thousands of gallons of water. The first supplies of fixed tanks were distributed to local authorities during 1939. They were five thousand gallon steel tanks built up with flanged steel sheets, and could be assembled easily. With small modifications the steel sheets could be used to construct tanks of almost any capacity. In peacetime it had been difficult to find suitable sites. After the onset of war some storage tanks had been set up in school playgrounds. When the bombing began, more large water tanks were established where wrecked houses had been cleared away. In January 1942 it was agreed that the London County Council should erect a large 'static water supply basin' on part of 'the Avenues' clearance area between Fulham Road and Burnthwaite Road. At their meeting on January 17 the Civil Defence Committee was informed that thirteen thousand men were likely to be available for training as Fire Guards. Fire bomb huts were to be erected at a number of suitable sites in Fulham so that the Fire Guards could be taught how to get through a smoke-filled room.

The provision of air-raid shelters was under constant revision in spite of the lull in the bombing. It was generally felt that the German bombers would be back once the Russian campaign ended. A new two-tier Morrison shelter was introduced which provided double the capacity of the standard Morrison. Three railway arches at Parsons Green Station were approved for use as air-raid shelters. People regarded these solidly-built arches as giving good protection from bombs. There were shelters under both the North and the South railway arches where the railway crosses the New Kings Road. Unfortunately, pilfering from shelters of such things as lamps still necessitated the locking of most shelters during the day.

Shortages of materials were increasingly affecting everyday life. Because of a shortage of shipping space, imports of paper for newspapers had been drastically reduced and the quality of the paper was poor. Each newspaper was allocated only a fixed amount of paper. Popular daily newspapers sometimes appeared with as few as four pages, and were quickly sold out because of the limited numbers printed. On 9 February 1942 soap rationing was introduced. The weekly ration varied according to the type of soap product, but was the equivalent of three ounces of toilet soap. The decision to ration soap was precipitated by the rapid advance of the Japanese in Malaysia after Pearl Harbour. This seemed likely to result in a shortage of palm oil which was important in the manufacture of soap. Food rationing arrangements in general remained unchanged. Under lend-lease arrangements a canned luncheon meat called Spam was being imported from the United States. Nobody seemed to have heard of this product before, but by the end of the War it was widely sold and Spam had become a household word. Canned rabbit from Australia was not so successful.

The next big change in food control came at the beginning of April when the production of white bread was stopped. Only wheatmeal bread could be sold. Two main factors had brought things to a head. The first was that a number of flour mills had been destroyed by bombing so that it had become necessary to import some flour. The second factor was the heavy sinking of American ships by U-boats off the east coast of the United States. These serious losses continued for some months until a convoy system was organized. The introduction of compulsory wheatmeal bread was generally accepted without either complaint or enthusiasm. Yet again it was a case of 'there's a war on'.

The increasing of national savings, to draw money out of circulation and reduce inflationary pressures, continued to be of vital importance. In Fulham the week of 21-28 March 1942 was to be Warship Week. The object was to raise £700,000 to pay for the new destroyer 'Relentless'. During the savings campaign there were various meetings organized to stimulate interest, and one speaker made the point that 'Large numbers of Fulhamites have during the past few months become income tax payers for the first time in their lives'. This was true because wages had risen considerably, and the income tax exemption rate had been lowered. Military bands played at Walham Green throughout the week and there were processions through the streets, with loud hailers urging people to save. The week was a success, with £932,401 being invested in national savings in Fulham. At the same time many people shared the feelings expressed by somebody who wrote in a local newspaper: 'Most of us have had enough talk and music through loud speakers to ensure that we shall look forward to a quieter existence when the week is over.'

An important local development in March was the completion of the new thoroughfare from Cromwell Road in Kensington to North End Road. This had entailed the building of a wide bridge over the railway which formed Fulham's eastern boundary. The planned widening of Talgarth Road had to be deferred until after the War. The newly completed road could not be brought into use for six weeks because of a delay in the delivery of traffic lights for the new intersection at the North End Road. This was just one example of the growing shortages of goods of all types. There was close Government control of raw materials, which were being allocated in general only for use in producing war equipment. Factories which formerly made peacetime goods were engaged in war work.

One small example of the problems arising from shortages at that time arose in the Civil Defence canteens in Fulham. Cups began vanishing at such a rate, doubtless to replace breakages in peoples homes, that canteen cups had to be made a personal issue. Crockery was 'in very short supply', and was being made only in plain white.

Local authorities had been urged by the Government to organize 'Holidays at

Home', and with the coming of spring in 1942 arrangements were being completed. In Fulham there were to be bands and concerts in the parks, and dances both indoor and outdoor. Advertisements urged Fulham people to spend their holidays at home, and posters were displayed around the Borough giving details of the programmes. The object was not only to raise public morale but to reduce the demand for transport especially for trains. Large movements of war material and of troops were going on all the time throwing a considerable strain on the railway system, but many people felt in need of a 'real' holiday. The beaches and coastal roads of south and south-east England generally had numerous anti-invasion obstacles so it was necessary to choose a seaside holiday resort with care. Advertisements and posters were produced throughout the War carrying the message 'Is Your Journey Really Necessary'.

There was a continuing strong demand for allotments from Fulham people, and in May it was announced that Polo Ground No. 1 at the Hurlingham Club was to be made available for this purpose. The Ministry of Food was continually issuing advertisements and posters concerning food production, a standard slogan being 'Dig for Victory'. By the end of the War it was estimated that ten per cent of the vegetables and fruit grown in Britain was produced in allotments and back gardens. The news of allotments at the Hurlingham Club prompted a nostalgic letter to one of the national newspapers. The writer said that before the War there had been an annual 'Indian Empire and the East' garden party at Hurlingham. Queen Mary had attended the last one in the summer of 1939. Polo Ground No. 2 continued in use for anti-aircraft guns, searchlights and barrage balloons.

Ways and means of saving fuel were under consideration continually. Before the War it had been common for grocers to deliver foodstuffs to their customers' homes. Early in 1942 a Government order was issued requiring deliveries to be restricted to a one-mile radius of any shop. Later in the year a zoning scheme was introduced for biscuit manufacturers who were allowed to supply their products only within a given distance of the factory. Jacobs Biscuits placed advertisements in the Fulham newspapers regretting that their cream crackers would not be available in Fulham again until after the end of hostilities. In general, transport operators were being encouraged to 'pool' transport in order to save petrol. In June the Government stopped the supply of petrol to private motorists except for some special categories such as doctors.

At their meeting on April 10 the Civil Defence Committee agreed the locations of the new incendiary bomb huts for training Fire Guards. The huts were to be at: (i) 12-14 Barton Road (bomb site); (ii) Lillie Road Recreation Ground; (iii) Bramber Road; (iv) Fulham Park Gardens; (v) Eelbrook Common. In December it was decided to have five additional huts so as to speed up the training of Fire Guards. These huts were to be on bomb sites at: (i) 109-111 Rannoch Road; (ii) 35-39 Danehurst Street; (iii) 54-60 Farm Lane (in a subsequent change of plan this site was in fact used for an emergency water tank while the fire hut was erected on the site of 41-45 Farm Lane); (iv) 11-13 Cristowe Road; and (v) South Park.

With the war situation looking more menacing the Government had decided in January 1942 that the conscription age for men to go into the armed services should be raised to fifty. Single girls aged 20-30 were also liable for conscription. In April Government notification was received that Fulham had to reduce the number of people allocated to the First Aid Posts to sixty-two. Of these, not more than one in four was to be a man. A month later a further directive stated that the number of full-time Air Raid Wardens was to be reduced by twenty per cent. The Minister of Labour's observation eight months earlier concerning the redeployment of labour necessary for a greater war effort was producing continuous results.

Many military camps were now under construction, or planned, to accommodate the large numbers of American troops who would soon be arriving. As a result there was a growing demand for building labour. Fulham Borough Council was informed that it would no longer be possible to direct men to Fulham to help with air-raid damage repairs.

Although there was no current risk of a German invasion it was thought likely that an attempt would be made once the Russian campaign had ended. The Home Guard in Fulham was given regular training, either locally or on Wimbledon Common or Hounslow Heath. The Fulham Civil Defence Committee, at their meeting on May 22, agreed to a Home Guard request to carry out exercises in and near Kenneth Road. This road was situated where Normand Park was developed after the War. The houses in and around Kenneth Road were derelict, having been badly damaged by the parachute mine which came down during the night of 16/17 October 1940. One noticeable feature of bomb sites throughout London was rose bay willow herb. This flower establishes itself easily on waste and burnt ground, and soon spreads. The mauvish pink flowers were a common sight by the end of the War, and helped to soften the ugliness of destruction.

The German attack on Russia made that country an ally of Britain, and large supplies of British war materials were convoyed to Murmansk. The Communist Party in Britain increased its membership, and began a long campaign for a Second Front to take the strain off the Russians. Advertisements appeared regularly in the Fulham newspapers, inserted by the London District Communist Party, urging a 'Second Front Now'. This slogan was also painted or chalked up on blank walls in the Borough as it was in towns throughout Britain.

No doubt everybody would have been glad to see a Second Front, but the hard fact was that the Germans had constructed many strong and skilfully sited fortifications all along the European coast. Many more ships and huge supplies of weapons and ammunition would need to be produced. A large American army would have to be trained and brought to England before an attack could be made, strong enough to break into German controlled Europe.

A British Soviet Commemoration Day was organized to be held at the Empress Hall in Fulham on Saturday 20 June 1942. This Hall was in Lillie Road near the Kensington boundary. It was demolished in the late nineteen-fifties and replaced by the Empress State Building. The Commemoration Day had the full support and patronage of the Prime Minister. The Soviet Ambassador attended. The Mayor of Fulham was invited to go, and spoke not only on behalf of the citizens of Fulham but also for the whole of London. Fulham supplied the Civil Defence contingent to take part in a pageant with detachments of the armed forces.

On Saturday November 7 there was another Russian celebration at the Empress Hall similar to the one in June. It was to celebrate the twenty-fifth anniversary of the Russian Revolution. Once again the Mayor of Fulham was invited to attend and to act as Chairman of the gathering.

In July the Civil Defence Committee received a Government circular emphasizing 'the important part to be played by local authorities' in the event of an invasion. During the weekend of September 5-6 an anti-invasion exercise code-named 'Southdown' was carried out in Fulham. Army units acted as German invaders. Some Wardens Posts were captured. The four main Civil Defence depots in Fulham at Cobbs Hall, Walham Green Baths, West Kensington Central School and New Kings Road at the end of Munster Road were captured one by one. It was possible to get most of the vehicles away from the depots, the objective being to move them into Chelsea. In connection with the plans to deal with an invasion, the Government asked that one house in each street should have a room allocated for use as a local first aid station.

In a statement in the House of Commons on 30 July 1942 Herbert Morrison announced that the Government no longer regarded the carrying of gas masks by the public as necessary. He went on to say that if the carrying of a mask 'was conclusive proof of the good citizenship of the men and women of this country, we should have to come to the conclusion that there were not many good citizens.' The public were asked to keep their masks easily accessible in their homes. Local authorities were told that the Government wished to emphasize 'with all the force at their command' that they did not consider that the risk of gas attack had passed.

Late in the summer there was another savings campaign, extending over ten weeks, to raise the level of savings locally. This enterprise was given the name 'Tanks for Attack'. The intention was to increase savings by at least twenty per cent compared with the same period of the previous year. To help publicize the event a garden party was held in the grounds of Fulham Palace. Some three hundred people attended and were addressed by both the Bishop of London and the Mayor of Fulham. The ten weeks campaign brought in £143,000 of national savings, making Fulham's total twenty-five per cent higher than in the previous year.

In August the Borough Engineer reported that the replacement of broken glass in windows throughout Fulham was behind the planned programme. The problem was still the great difficulty in obtaining supplies of glass. The blast effect from bombs had shattered huge numbers of windows in Britain's towns, and the glass manufacturers were unable to cope with the demand. During the bombing it had been necessary to replace windows with glass substitutes which were thin and gave poor insulation. These materials could be difficut to cut, and as a result the new panes were not always well fitted. Some shopkeepers had boarded up their windows leaving only the central part with glass. The wood surrounds were usually painted, sometimes with gay patterns. Fifty per cent of the new glass being supplied was not transparent but was an 'obscure' type of war-time glass. The policy followed in Fulham was to concentrate on re-glazing windows in the rooms most used. Later in the year supplies of glass improved, and a considerable effort was made to complete the most essential re-glazing before the onset of winter.

The Government had been urging the utmost economy in using light and heat, and during the summer a Ministry of Fuel was established. Preparations for fuel rationing had to be made, and Fulham's Fuel Office was established in St Johns Hall at Walham Green. The basic form of heating in Fulham at that time was by coal fires. At the beginning of October, advertisements appeared in the local newspapers stating that 'From 1st August to 31 October you may not order more than one ton of coal or increase your stock to more than one-and-a-half tons'. At the end of October further advertisements intimated that every householder was required to complete a copy of a fuel assessment form which was being issued by the local fuel office. The labour force in the coal mines had fallen by ten per cent from the 1939 figure. Earlier in the War many young miners had left the then poorly paid coal industry to go into better paid work in war factories. By 1942 coal production had fallen by about ten per cent from its pre-war level. Factory demand for coal was rising, and eventually domestic users as a whole received only two-thirds of their pre-war consumption.

In October a Ministry of Home Security refresher course on poison gas was attended by a representative from Fulham. In their guidance the Ministry emphasized that 'there is still a very real danger that gas may be used, at least as a final resort, when the enemy is on the verge of defeat'. Earlier in the year a special check had been made of the gas masks of all the 6506 children who were then attending school in Fulham. It was found that 1816 of the masks needed repairs or even complete replacement.

It was still thought that future air raids would bring a greater fire hazard than ever, and many additional water supply reservoirs were being constructed in Fulham. In October new arrangements were agreed for co-operation between Fire Guards and the National Fire Service. To obviate numerous telephone calls to the Fire Service the Fire Guards were to report only fires that they could not deal with themselves. A Fire Guard was to cycle to the nearest Fire Station to make the report. The locations of the Fire Stations were recorded in October 1942 as: (i) 685 Fulham Road (main station); (ii) Beaufort House School; (iii) Ackmar Road School; (iv) Townmead Road; (v) Finlay Street Secondary School; (vi) Everington Street School; (vii) St Dunstans Road School. On Saturday and Sunday, October 3 and October 4, women aged 20-45 were required to register for fire watching. It was estimated that some twenty-five thousand women registered in Fulham, but large numbers were able to claim exemption because of responsibilities such as the care of young children. Some day nurseries were being opened locally in adapted premises to help free young mothers for part-time duties of one sort or another.

In the middle of November the Civil Defence Committee was informed that the Fire Guard strength in Fulham then totalled 5546 men and 6504 women. Of these, nearly a hundred were aliens. Their enrolment shows the big change in attitude towards aliens since the worried days of 1940. In general the arrangements for the new Fire Guard seem to have worked satisfactorily. Occasionally, and reluctantly, a summons had to be issued when somebody would not attend the necessary training sessions. It was at this time that instructions were received to collect in all the sandmats and sandbins which had been placed around Fulham. During 1941 the enemy had introduced a new type of one kilogram incendiary. This had a small pellet of penthrite, a particularly powerful explosive, attached to it. The heat of the burning incendiary set off the penthrite. This could injure anybody nearby, as well as distributing the burning magnesium more widely. In 1942 an even more dangerous incendiary appeared. Penthrite was contained inside the tubular steel head, and when it exploded the fragments of steel could kill up to a range of fifty yards. Sand was ineffective against these explosive incendiaries unless used in very large amounts. The stirrup pump remained the best antidote for incendiaries.

Alderman Gentry had to relinquish the post of Chief Warden in November because of ill health. Councillor T. Horton then became Acting Chief Warden, and was made Chief Warden in July 1943. He occupied this post until the end of the War.

The new ration books to come into force in July 1942 were issued in May, and on this occasion they were available at the public libraries in Fulham as well as the Methodist Hall at Walham Green. In May the Fulham Food Control Committee received an application from the women on their staff to be allowed to wear slacks on duty. Slacks and a head scarf were then commonly worn by younger women as a means of conserving clothing coupons. 'Utility' standards for clothing manufacture were laid down by the Government to make the most economical use of materials and labour. Clothes in the shops were generally satisfactory, but stockings in particular were criticized as being of poor quality. Most members of the Food Committee disliked the idea of their staff wearing slacks, but had to agree. The Ministry of Food had agreed and the staff were civil servants employed by the Ministry.

On June 24 dried eggs became available on points in the shops. The Ministry of Food organized a publicity campaign to explain how the new product could be used, and dried eggs proved a considerable success. The allocation of shell eggs remained very low especially during the winter. People who wished to keep a few chickens could forgo their egg allocation and obtain a ration of 'balancer meal' instead to help feed the hens. A month after the introduction of dried eggs the rationing of sweets and chocolates was introduced. The ration was two ounces a week, and remained at this level until some years after the War.

In general the system of food rationing had settled down to an established pattern. Meals in canteens and restaurants were supplied without the use of food coupons, an arrangement which continued in force throughout the War. In fact, barely two per cent of all the food consumed in Britain was provided in these establishments, but it was a welcome extra. Meat supplies were restricted and in October all Civil Defence canteens were required to have two meatless days a week. The number of stalls in the North End Road had become noticeably fewer than in pre-war days, and there were far fewer men among the stall-holders.

A scheme was being worked out to have only one milkman deliver in each road instead of two or three as was then general. The main object was to save labour. Milk supply remained a problem, because after the priority classes had taken up their allocations there was never enough to meet the general demand. The seasonal fall in milk production during the winter months always accentuated the difficulty. In December 1942 the non-priority milk ration was reduced to two pints a week and even this could not be guaranteed.

German bombers did not attack London during 1942 but made sporadic raids on various provincial towns. On May 30 the R.A.F. made a night raid on Cologne using one thousand bombers, the first time this figure had been reached in a single attack. It was sensational news. More thousand bomber raids on German towns were to follow.

Commonwealth forces achieved a decisive victory over the German army in North Africa at the Battle of Alamein which ended on November 4. In December a larger German army was surrounded by the Russians at Stalingrad, and was trapped. The surrender came in January 1943.

The War had already lasted well over three years and it was impossible to forecast how much longer it would go on. The local newspapers often carried reports of Fulham men killed, and inevitably people gradually became hardened to the news of these deaths. One local impact of the War had come in August, following a raid on Dieppe by a strong force of Canadian troops. There had been heavy casualties, and some of the wounded had been brought to Fulham Hospital and to the Western Hospital in Seagrave Road.

Canadian troops had been in England since the early days of the War and were stationed in the south of the country. They had long been a familiar sight in London. During 1942 the first of what was to be a huge American army arrived. They were a novelty with their somewhat dapper uniforms and Hollywood film accents. Before the days of television the general impression of Americans had been derived largely from the cinema.

Christmas 1942 was quiet and meals had to be comparatively frugal. In the long blacked-out winter evenings radio had become of prime importance as a means of entertainment. A light-hearted programme called ITMA (It's that man again) had established itself as the most popular comedy feature. Tommy Handley, a Liverpool comedian who headed the cast, became a national figure. He was invited to Windsor Castle with his company to meet the King.

There was also a thoughtful side to life. A widespread urge for social reform had grown stronger during the War. On December 1 there was published a Report by Sir William Beveridge outlining a plan for comprehensive social security. It was warmly welcomed by most people and sold in large numbers. Also during the War Mr R.A. Butler was working away on a thorough reform of the educational system of England and Wales. It is said that his work was helped by the experiences of many middle-class people in caring for evacuated children. The ignorance and bad behaviour of some of these children came as a shock. Mr Butler's efforts culminated in the important Education Act of 1944.

CHAPTER EIGHT
WAITING FOR D-DAY: JANUARY 1943-JUNE 1944

AT their meeting on 4 January 1943 the Civil Defence Committee was informed that the number of Air Raid Wardens in Fulham had been reduced from its earlier establishment of three hundred to 243. Of these, sixty-seven were women. The number of part-time Wardens had been increased from five hundred to 647. These changes resulted from constant efforts to make the best possible use of the nation's manpower. Young women were being directed, not only into the armed forces but also into war work. This latter requirement sometimes necessitated their being required to go to some other part of the country. Occasionally a woman would decline to comply with a directive and a prosecution would follow. Instances were reported in Fulham of women being unwilling to move away to such places as Coventry or Stafford. Usually their protests were not accepted, and they had to comply with the law. As with rationing, the general public accepted these compulsions as being necessary.

The numerous emergency water storage tanks sometimes sustained damage, either accidental or deliberate. It was decided that walls should be built round them as a protection. Barbed wire was fixed round the top. This was partly to stop boys clambering up with the risk of accidental drowning. It was also hoped that the barbed wire would make it more difficult for people to throw rubbish into the tanks.

The shortage of replacement glass continued, and a new Government directive asked local authorities to replace only half the glass in living rooms and kitchens. Windows in bedrooms were to be left boarded up. Many had in fact been boarded up for two years.

On Sunday night January 17, German bombers made their first large-scale attack on London since 10 May 1941. The main targets were the Millwall and Woolwich dock areas. There were no bombs in Fulham that night, but four anti-aircraft shells came down south of the New Kings Road. Three of them exploded. One was in the roadway opposite 4 Chipstead Street where two Wardens and another man were standing. One of the Wardens was killed. Two other shells fell in back gardens, one in the garden of 48 Perrymead Street and the other in that of 19 Chipstead Street. The latter did not explode. The fourth shell exploded at a wharf in Townmead Road.

Food continued to be an everyday pre-occupation. There had been a good potato harvest the previous year, and Ministry of Food advertisements urged people to eat more potatoes and less bread. A cartoon character 'Potato Pete' was devised to help the campaign. An interesting development in January was the granting of a licence to a Belgian to sell horseflesh at a shop in New Kings Road.

At the beginning of February it was announced that a new Londoners Meal Service centre was to be established in the former Timothy Davies premises at 2-6 Fulham Broadway. This became known as the Granville Restaurant. In 1940 the Ministry of Food had decided to encourage local authorities to establish communal feeding centres. It was considered that the upheavals of war had made such centres desirable. Many people had been evacuated and ever-increasing numbers of women were working in factories. It would be possible to obtain a hot nutritious meal in these centres at a reasonable price. Developments were slow except in London where the bombing in the autumn of 1940 stimulated action. The London County Council was responsible for these centres in London, and the first one was opened on the Isle of Dogs in the East End on 15 September 1940. Within a fortnight the L.C.C. had fifty operating, mostly in heavily bombed areas. In March 1941, at the suggestion of Winston Churchill, the name British Restaurant was given to the meals centres.

Several of these establishments were opened in Fulham, mostly in schools. At one time or another there were British Restaurants in William Street School which was rebuilt as Avonmore School; Kingwood Road School later part of Henry Compton School; North End Road School, and the Marist Convent next to Fulham Library. There was also one in part of Fulham Hospital, particularly useful because Fulham Palace Road School opposite the Hospital was the main rest centre for bombed-out people.

By 1943 so many children were back in London that numerous schools were being re-opened. This necessitated the removal of British Restaurants from school premises and their replacement elsewhere. The one in North End Road School, for example, was transferred to the Bethel Chapel at the corner of North End Road and Chesson Road. The Marist Convent Restaurant was closed when the new one was opened at 2-6 Fulham Broadway. This closure was much regretted locally. The Convent meals were regarded as being of particularly good quality and the service was not the cafeteria type. Food was brought to the table. Many British Restaurants continued to operate for some years after the War.

The bombers came back to London in some force on the night of March 3. Eight high explosive bombs fell in Fulham, all in the south of the Borough. Three fell in the grounds of Fulham Palace, causing some damage to the buildings. There was a disaster that night in Bethnal Green. When the sirens sounded, a large number of people began descending the staircase of the new Underground Station there. As the bombers approached, a rocket battery in a nearby park fired a salvo of rockets. These so-called Z-batteries never had much success and were not widely used. The 'whoosh' of the rockets startled the Bethnal Green shelterers and they surged forward. In a matter of seconds there was a huge pile-up of people. When the mass of bodies was finally cleared it was found that 178 had died. After this, modifications were made to Underground Station entrances to prevent a repetition of such a tragedy. As was normal policy, no public announcement was made at the time but the news soon spread. In fact, after any night of bombing, Londoners soon heard if a particular area had been hard hit.

At their meeting on March 1 the Civil Defence Committee received a report on the progress of re-glazing in Fulham. During the three months of December 1942, and January and February 1943, 34,750 square feet of glass had been fitted to windows in the Borough. This was a little more than in the previous three months when 30,500 square feet had been put in. One regrettable result of the air raids was that people were often claiming that their houses had sustained bomb damage when in fact normal deterioration was the problem. The Civil Defence Committee decided that a deposit of thirty shillings should be charged if a roof had to be inspected. This would be forfeited if a surveyor reported that the roof had not sustained damage as a result of bombing and the owner was simply 'trying it on'. Although every effort was made to control the situation, there is no doubt that a considerable amount of so-called air-raid damage, rectified at Government expense, was the result of past neglect. Agents set themselves up in business, offering to handle damage claims in return for a percentage of the money they obtained.

As the winter drew to a close there were a number of exercises in Fulham involving the Civil Defence services and sometimes the Home Guard. The latter operated mainly in yet another anti-invasion exercise in which army units took the part of enemy troops advancing into Fulham from the south. The Civil Defence services were exercised in several ways. Beaumont Mansions in the West Kensington area had suffered bomb damage, and the Rescue Parties exercised there. Arrangements were made for some children to be inside and to call for help. The exercise began realistically enough with the children groaning noisily, but after a time they became bored and began singing loudly. In a damaged house in Kenneth Road a big fire was started, and the Auxiliary Fire Service was called to deal with it. In Rigault Road, by Fulham High Street, tear gas bombs were used and the Civil Defence services operated with gas masks. Notice of the exercises had been given previously. The Government was still very alert to the possibility of poison gas being used. At the beginning of March, Fulham's Civil Defence Committee was informed by the London Civil Defence Commissioners that a Gas Identification Officer should always be available in the Control Room. It would be the Officer's responsibility to investigate any suspicion that gas was being used and to identify the type.

Early in March there was another national savings drive in Fulham using the slogan 'Wings for Victory'. The object was to raise £700,000, this being the same target figure as in Warship Week held twelve months previously. 'Wings for Victory' week began on Saturday March 6 and ended on Saturday March 13. The former Timothy Davies premises were again used for an exhibition, this time entitled 'A Day With the R.A.F.'. An aircraft from the First World War was on display, lent by the Science Museum, and there was also the casing of a five hundred pound bomb. A notice said that this was going to be filled with explosive and dropped on Berlin. Throughout the week, detachments of the Civil Defence units and of the Home Guard had marched around Fulham with bands playing. The smartness of the Home Guard attracted much favourable comment. The climax to Wings for Victory was a march past the Town Hall on the final Saturday afternoon by an army detachment from Chelsea Barracks. The Mayor, Councillor P. Barton, was to take the salute on the balcony. Unfortunately the army arrived unexpectedly fifteen minutes early, and the Mayor had not gone up to the balcony. He had time only to get to the steps of the ground floor entrance in Harwood Road and the army gave a smart 'eyes right' to an empty balcony. Financially the week was a great success. Fulham people contributed £1,127,000 to national savings, far exceeding the target figure.

Wages had by now considerably outstripped price rises. There was some grumbling at the high wages being offered to boys and girls aged fourteen to eighteen. As soon as they reached the latter age they could be directed into the armed services or war industries. Quite apart from the special savings weeks, organized in turn in specific localities, there was a continuous Government advertising campaign urging people to save. Both the press and the cinema were used. Cartoon advertisements in newspapers urged people to save, while an obnoxious little figure called 'Squander Bug' was shown using his wiles to persuade them to spend.

Another Government campaign operating throughout the War concerned security and the need not to talk carelessly of any matters in which the enemy might be interested. 'Be like dad, keep mum' and 'Careless talk costs lives' were favourite slogans. Cartoon advertisements in the newspapers and on posters showed two 'gossips' on a bus, while behind them listening intently were Hitler and Marshall Goering, Commander in Chief of the German Air Force.

New ration books, to come into force in July, were issued over a period of weeks from the end of May. Fulham people could collect their new books either at the Baptist Church Hall in Dawes Road, or at any of the libraries. The ration books included not only sweet coupons but also the clothing ration book as a detachable insert. As things turned out there were to be no further fundamental changes in the rationing system during the remaining years of the War. The pattern of ration book introduced for 1943-44 remained basic for the next three years. The new books for children had pages printed to control the allocation of oranges. This fruit still reached Britain only occasionally and in small shipments. A typical allocation would be one pound of oranges for each child. Fruit such as bananas and pineapples had not been imported since 1940, and children were growing up who could not remember such exotic luxuries.

On Sunday June 20 a barrage balloon from the site at Queensmill School caught fire. Burning pieces fell in the area of Queensmill Road, Lysia Street, Woodlawn Road and Holyport Road. Fortunately as it was Sunday there were plenty of people available with stirrup pumps to deal with the fires. Only a few minor casualties resulted.

In the second half of June there were problems over meat supply. Butchers were receiving good supplies of pork but not much other meat. All customers were asked to accept part pork for their ration which inevitably caused some irritation. The weather was very hot, and in those days very few people had refrigerators. In fact the Ministry of Food had been engaged for several weeks in tough negotiations with the Argentine Government over new meat contracts. This may have led the Ministry to husband meat stocks pending the outcome of the negotiations.

In the middle of July a Report on the future planning of London was issued. It had been prepared by Professor Abercrombie, a distinguished authority in the field of town planning. Various recommendations were made concerning Fulham. The Chelsea Embankment should be continued along the riverside to Wandsworth Bridge. A new road link to the embankment should be constructed, following the line of the railway on Fulham's eastern boundary. Professor Abercrombie also recommended that the riverside industries north of Fulham Palace should be removed so as to open up a riverside walk. He wanted more public use made of the two large private open spaces in Fulham, namely the grounds of Fulham Palace and of the Hurlingham Club. Some of the changes recommended have taken place. At the time of writing, the Hammersmith and Fulham Borough Council has Fulham Palace and its grounds on long lease. The industrial riverside north of Fulham Palace has been transformed. The industries that were there have mostly gone and have been replaced by residential development with access along the riverside.

The Preparatory Department of Lady Margaret School had re-opened at Parsons Green after Easter. The School had been in use for the Auxiliary Fire Service. During the summer it was announced that the entire school would return from Midhurst in time for the September term. During the long lull in the bombing some parents had brought their daughters back from Midhurst and enrolled them in other schools. By this time a large proportion of Fulham child evacuees had come home, although some parents still preferred their children to remain in a safe area.

Women with young children were being given every encouragement and help to work in war industries or transport. Fulham's fifth wartime day nursery was opened in temporary premises in Jervis Road in July. There was separate accommodation for babies (up to eighteen months), tweenies (eighteen months to 2½ years) and toddlers (2½ to five years). The peak of wartime mobilisation was reached at the end of the summer in 1943. Of the thirty-three million people in Britain aged between fourteen and sixty-four, twenty-two million were then engaged in either the armed forces, civil defence, industry or transport.

The danger of stocks of food being contaminated by poison gas had long been recognized, and methods of dealing with such a situation had been devised and tested. At the end of October a large-scale demonstration was held in the grounds of the Hurlingham Club to show what could be done to 'clean' contaminated food. Eight hundred food decontamination officers attended from all over Britain, and Lord Woolton came to watch. He was the Minister of Food and had been brought into the Government from the world of private business early in the War.

More and more units of the United States army had been arriving in Britain, and American soldiers were to be seen everywhere. At their meeting on November 1, Fulham's Civil Defence Committee received a request to make some space available for American soliders in Queens Club. This was needed for gymnastics, physical training and boxing. Fulham Borough Council had leased the entire premises to accommodate Civil Defence stores, furniture from bombed premises and a section of the Women's Voluntary Service. One empty warehouse area occupying thirteen thousand square feet was held in reserve for emergencies. It was agreed that this should be made available for the Americans, but should be relinquished immediately if required.

Saturday night November 7 brought tragedy just across the river in Putney High Street. It was not unusual for the air raid sirens to sound when there might be only one or two bombers droning round over London. People had long since learnt to live with this situation, and most of them carried on more or less normally. At 11 p.m. a bomb crashed down on a crowded dance hall at the junction of Putney Bridge Road and Putney High Street. Well over a hundred people died including many young women from Fulham. The following week was a sad one locally with funeral processions making their way through various parts of the Borough.

On the following night two bombs fell in the south of Fulham. One was on a commercial garage in Wandsworth Bridge Road. The other fell in South Park close to its eastern boundary. Settrington Road backs on to the Park, and 270 houses were damaged in the vicinity. The powerful blast of the bomb brought large numbers of slates off the roofs, and eighteen thousand of them had to be replaced.

With the approach of Christmas 1943 more children were being brought back from the evacuation areas by their parents. Fulham Central School for Boys had been evacuated to Haslemere in 1939 and had remained there ever since. Late in 1943 the London County Council decided that the time had come for it to come back to Fulham. The boys who had been living at Haslemere for four years seem to have had a happy time with their country hosts. Many families in Fulham spoke warmly of the kindness shown to their children.

At Christmas the giving of presents was difficult because there was so little to buy. Many shops opened only on certain days of the week because they had nothing much to sell. Many simple household utensils such as kettles and saucepans were virtually unobtainable. People were advertising for second-hand bicycles, vacuum cleaners and other things which could not be bought new.

During 1943 the Allied armies had driven the German forces out of North Africa. On July 9 the Allies invaded Sicily. Later that month Mussolini was removed from office by decision of the Italian Grand Council and on September 7 the Italian Government signed an armistice. The Germans then sent reinforcements to their army in Italy ready to hold the country against the Allies.

Also in 1943 British and American bombers had been carrying out increasingly heavy attacks on Germany. This mass bombing destroyed extensive areas of the large cities, and was no longer claimed to be precision bombing. Some people felt deeply concerned and criticized the strategy. The Bishop of Chichester, George Bell, spoke out several times. In the House of Lords in October 1943 he said: 'To bomb cities as cities, deliberately to attack civilians quite irrespective of whether they were contributing to the war effort, is a wrong deed whether done by the Nazis or by ourselves.'

In November 1943 Hitler gave orders that there were to be reprisal attacks against England. London was to be the primary target. The German bomber force in the west was at a low ebb, and the Germans withdrew all the air strength they could spare from the Mediterranean and Russian fronts. It was intended to make considerable use of incendiary bombs. A new type of container had been devised which could hold as many as 620 of these devices. At intervals during its fall the layers of incendiaries would be released to give an even spread over a large area.

The main attacks on London started on January 21 and continued intermittently until the end of March. Fulham's turn came late on the evening of Sunday February 20. In less than one hour twenty high explosive bombs fell as well as an estimated seven thousand incendiaries. The official record says that 'less than half' the incendiaries ignited, but these 'caused twelve serious fires and a great number of lesser fires dealt with by Fire Guards'. The furniture from bombed-out houses stored at Queens Club caught fire and there was a spectacular blaze. New arrangements had to be made for such furniture. At one time and another use was made of the closed Grand Theatre by Putney Bridge, shop premises at 1-10 Jerdan Place and Fulham Council's premises at 122-126 New Kings Road for storing furniture. A large proportion of the incendiaries contained explosive devices, something of which the Fire Guards had been warned. They had to take extra care when approaching a blazing incendiary in case it should blow up.

There was some concentration of high explosive bombs in the West Kensington and Barons Court areas, and along the riverside. North End Road School was severely damaged and caught fire. The Home Guard had a Company Headquarters in the school, and quantities of hand grenades, detonators and fuses were hurriedly removed from the burning building. Subsequently the Home Guard established its replacement Company Headquarters in Lillie Road School. Bombs falling in the vicinity of North End Road School resulted in the deaths of fourteen people. Although of such short duration the effects of the bombing in Fulham that night had been serious. А total of seventy-six people had been killed and 194 were detained in hospital. Ninety-five houses had been demolished or badly damaged, and another 2,500 houses had suffered damage in varying degrees. The rest centres were crowded with people whose homes were uninhabitable. Fulham Palace Road School was still the main centre for the homeless.

At the junction of North End Road and Lillie Road a container of incendiaries landed in the roadway. It had failed to open during its descent, and caused an explosion sufficient to split open the roadway and set a gas main alight. Three phosphorus incendiary bombs, falling at various places in Fulham, all failed to explode and were cleared away some days later. Phosphorus bombs had been introduced by the enemy in 1942 but this is the first record of their falling in Fulham. Identical in shape with the small (50 kg) high explosive bomb, the original phosphorus bombs were filled with a mixture of phosphorus, crude oil, wood shavings and other incendiary material. As soon as the phosphorus was exposed to the air the filling burst into flames. By 1944 the contents of phosphorus bombs had been changed and consisted of a sticky mixture of phosphorus and rubber. In general, these bombs do not seem to have been very effective. A parabomb in the Hurlingham Club grounds also failed to explode, and was recorded as having been the first unexploded parabomb in the London Region. Part of Rivermead Court had to be evacuated. Parabombs were delayed action bombs which floated down on parachutes.

There was some feeling in Fulham that bombs falling in the West Kensington and Barons Court areas were intended for St Pauls School which was situated in

Hammersmith just across from Fulham's northern boundary. The School was a large building facing Hammersmith Road, and it suffered a good deal of bomb damage during the War. The boys had been evacuated to Easthampstead in Berkshire on the outbreak of hostilities, and the Army took over the building. Eventually it became the Headquarters of the 21st Army Group which was responsible for planning the invasion of Europe. A study of the exact points at which bombs fell in Hammersmith on that evening of February 20 does not support the theory that St Pauls School was the intended target. Many officers working at the School were billetted in flats in West Kensington and Barons Court. Perhaps they were the target.

On Wednesday evening February 23, Fulham had another short 'hammering' which started soon after 10.30 p.m. and was all over within half-an-hour. A line of four high explosive bombs in the north-west corner of Fulham resulted in numerous casualties, both dead and injured. Many houses were destroyed. Two heavy bombs caused particular devastation. One fell in the centre of Skelwith Road some way west of the junction with Rannoch Road. The other was recorded as having fallen at 15-31 Chancellors Road. In the centre of the Borough, in Felden Street and other streets just north of it, there was a concentration of incendiaries. The explosive type caused a number of casualties. There was a fatality in Felden Street caused by an exploding incendiary, and several people were injured by incendiaries in nearby Fernhurst Road and Radipole Road. In Reporton Road a woman was struck and killed by a falling incendiary. An incendiary bomb container, which had failed to open properly and still contained its load, landed on an air raid shelter in Rosaville Road killing five people. The biggest fire was at the riverside in the Shell Mex Depot at Lensbury Wharf. It ranked in London terms as a major fire and forty appliances were directed there to bring the blaze under control. Explosions from the Depot could be heard all over the southern part of Fulham. Phosphorus incendiary bombs proved to be as ineffective as ever. One fell in Bishops Park and another in Fulham Cemetery. Neither could have done much harm in those locations, but in any case both failed to ignite. Something new in Fulham was an unrotated projectile which came down in the Gas Works having failed to explode at altitude. This was the type of rocket which had caused the alarm at Bethnal Green Underground Station the previous year. It was cleared away from the Gas Works a week later. These Z-battery projectiles were steel tubes about seven and a half feet long. There was a fuse in the head, a propellant in the tail, and a high explosive charge in the main length of the tube. When they fell the projectiles came down almost vertically and penetrated very deep. Bomb Disposal Units found them troublesome things to deal with. A total of ten high explosive bombs fell in Fulham that evening and fifty-five people were killed. Sixty had to be taken to hospital and detained there. Approximately two thousand people were rendered homeless. Eighty-four houses were wrecked or badly damaged, and 2300 others sustained some damage. The Germans were using much bigger bombs than had been the case earlier in the War. This must explain the considerable amount of damage.

The serious fire situation showed how right the authorities had been in carrying out a big expansion of the fire services. Unfortunately there were some bad citizens who did nothing to help but actually hindered. A good deal of rubbish was thrown into static water tanks, and this could easily choke hoses when water was being pumped out. There had been a thorough cleaning out of the tanks during the winter. The necessity for this was underlined by one particular example in Langford Road, Sands End. A tank there was found to contain an estimated seventeen tons of rubbish.

Three weeks after the raids nearly all the people made homeless had been rehoused although often only temporarily. Three hundred lorry loads of furniture had been collected from wrecked homes by the Borough Council and taken into store. Bombed-out people could get priority authorization to obtain such things as linen and towels. Otherwise the waiting period would have been intolerable. One of the directors of Barbers Stores in North End Road said at the time that there was 'usually twelve months wait to get a pair of sheets'. The allocation to the trade was only six per cent of pre-war supplies. Shortly afterwards the allocation was doubled and the waiting period for sheets was reduced to six months.

The attacks on London during February caused considerable damage and the Inspector General of Air Raid Precautions reported: 'A greater proportion of high calibre bombs was noted in these raids and there was a very appreciable increase in the blast effect they produced . . . The population are more jittery than they were in the old days due probably to a lot of contributory factors such as belief that we had air superiority and therefore no more attacks to fear; war-weariness; lack of stamina and so on. There were no signs of any panic, but the people seemed more helpless and more dependent on the Civil Defence services than they were in the old days. Everyone flocked to the Wardens posts with their troubles after the raid and wanted a good deal of helping. The effect of the handling of the homeless, and so on, by the Civil Defence services was most marked and quickly helped to get their tails up again, but they found a good deal of apathy.'

Following these sharp raids on the capital, building operatives were directed into London from other places to help with the massive work of repairs. Approximately 350 men came to Fulham from Birmingham. Twenty-five slaters and plasterers were directed from Glasgow by the Ministry of Works. Some building men came from other parts of London for varying periods, including 233 who were employed by two building firms in Stepney.

At their meeting on April 19 the Civil Defence Committee received a comprehensive report on the damage situation. The number of houses either already demolished or needing demolition as a result of the February raids totalled 277. This was rather worse than originally thought. First aid repairs had been carried out to 5450 homes. Once again the shortage of glass was proving a problem, and the glazing situation was described as 'quite serious'.

One useful innovation after each of the February raids was the setting up of an Incident Inquiry Point usually in the charge of an Air Raid Warden. A convenient place was chosen near the bombed area with a blue flag marking its location. People searching for relatives and friends, or needing help of any kind, could go to the Inquiry Point for assistance.

The general impression in Fulham was that the heavy casualties in these two

February raids were caused by the reluctance of many people to go to the air raid shelters in good time. There had been a long lull in the bombing. Many evacuees had come back from the safe areas, and most of the local schools had re-opened. All this resulted in a relaxed feeling that the worst was over. Only the more cautious took shelter as soon as the sirens sounded. The majority waited until they heard bombs nearby. Then it was too late.

King George and Queen Elizabeth had long made a practice of visiting badly bombed areas, and after the February raids they came to Fulham. They visited bombed-out people in the rest centres and went to see where the bombs had fallen. They spent some time in Skelwith Road where Heavy Rescue Parties were still at work. A few days later a royal gift arrive for distribution among people who had recently lost their homes. There were blankets, a load of tea and a hundredweight of honey.

German bombers made some more sharp attacks on London during the next four weeks but there was little damage in Fulham. Incendiaries were dropped in large numbers during each of the raids. On the night of March 14 the Congregational Church in Dawes Road was extensively damaged by fire caused by incendiaries. Numerous incendiaries fell in the central area of Fulham, with a concentration in the locality of Dawes Road, Gironde Road and Bishops Road. Many houses were damaged by fire and there was a fatality at 83 Dawes Road. The fire situation would have been much worse if it had not been for the work of the Fire Guards. One example of this was at Fulham Central Library where an incendiary crashed through the glass roof over the reference library and began burning fiercely inside. Fortunately the Fire Guards on duty, the Chief Librarian and a member of his staff, managed to extinguish the fire with a stirrup pump before the flames got a hold.

On the night of March 21/22 two unexploded U.P.s (unrotated projectiles) came down in Fulham just after one o'clock in the morning. The first one landed outside 47-51 Garvan Road with tragic results. Three Fire Guards were killed and six other people were seriously injured. Almost immediately afterwards the second U.P. crashed outside 15 Avonmore Road. Fortunately only one man was injured.

There was one more German attack of some consequence on London during April but Fulham was not affected. After that, the greatly reduced German air strength was concentrated on reconnaissance flights together with some bombing along the South Coast of England. It was obviously hoped that these tactics might interfere with Allied preparations to invade Europe.

From March 25 to April 1 another of the big savings campaigns was operated in Fulham. This one was called 'Salute the Soldier' and the target figure was £800,000. There was the familiar concentration of events at Fulham Broadway. A bandstand was set up and bands played daily. A tank and a gun stood close by,. The premises at 4-6 Fulham Broadway were not made available, as the British Restaurant was operating in them, but the gas showrooms were used for a display of army weapons and equipment. The showrooms were sited between Fulham Broadway and Vanston Place. By the end of the week £988,910 had been contributed to national savings in Fulham.

CHAPTER NINE

D-DAY AND AFTER: JUNE 1944-AUGUST 1945

B Y the first weekend in June, Fulham's Holidays at Home programme was in full swing. The weather was rather dull but many people were enjoying the concerts and entertainments in the parks. None of them knew that a minesweeping flotilla had sailed from the River Clyde on the Friday evening en route for the English Channel. Its task was to 'sweep' an approach channel to Normandy in readiness for the invasion of Europe. The first news of the invasion came on Tuesday morning 6 June 1944, which was to be another day of excitement comparable to 1 September 1939. For the next few days the war effort was concentrated in Normandy. There were no enemy aircraft over Britain.

The Government had known for some months, from intelligence reports, that the Germans were developing two new secret weapons. One was a pilotless aircraft laden with explosive, and the other a long-range rocket. British reconnaissance aircraft located the newly-constructed launching sites for the pilotless aircraft in North-West France. These sites were heavily bombed late in 1943 and in the early months of 1944. The Germans reacted by building simpler sites, heavily camouflaged and in woodland areas. The original German plan had been to start using their new weapon against London by December 1943, but the Allied counter-bombing made this impossible.

At last, a week after the D-Day landings in Normandy, the first flying bombs were launched towards England. This was in the early hours of Wednesday June 13. Ten flying bombs were fired and four of them reached this country. Three of the four came down in South-East England, but only one reached London. That fell in Stepney. The Cabinet had already decided that no public statement should be made concerning the new form of air warfare until the weight of the attack made it necessary. This was so as to deny the enemy any information as to the effects of the new weapon for as long as possible. The main onslaught began in the late evening of June 15 and continued throughout the night. A total of 244 flying bombs were fired that night, but many crashed in France or into the sea. Seventy-three reached the London area. The nation first learnt about the new weapon from the B.B.C. one o'clock news on June 16 when it was reported that the enemy had started using pilotless aircraft against this country. The name 'doodlebug' soon came into vogue, but at their meeting on June 19 the Cabinet decided on the name flying bomb.

The first flying bomb to come down in Fulham was in Lintaine Grove just before five o'clock on Sunday morning June 18. The records show that fifteen people were killed and twenty-nine seriously injured. The blast effect of the new weapon proved to be much greater than that of conventional high explosive bombs. The standard bomb, with its conical shape and pointed nose, hurtled downards at increasing speed. It 'dug' itself in before exploding, often making a large crater. The flying bomb came down like a small aircraft, its wings tending to steady its descent. It did not 'dig' into the ground so that its blast effect was mainly sideways. Broken glass was everywhere, and people approaching the scene of an incident had to shuffle along through the glass. Fulham's second flying bomb crashed on St Mary's Church, Hammersmith Road at 9.45 p.m. the same day. The church was completely destroyed. One person was killed and fourteen seriously injured. That Sunday had been a bad day in London with many flying bombs falling. The worst incident of all occurred in the morning when a flying bomb fell on the Guards Chapel at Wellington Barracks by St James Park. Sunday morning service was in progress and 119 people were killed. Others died later. No public announcement was made but, as usual, the news of such a tragedy soon spread throughout the capital.

During the next few days Fulham was fortunate. No flying bombs came down in the Borough, although rather more than fifty a day were reaching London. The majority of them were falling south of the Thames, with areas such as Croydon, Wandsworth and Lewisham receiving a large share. Some of the flying bombs actually fell in rural areas to the south of London, and it seems that in general they were slightly under-ranged. Fulham's third flying bomb came in Racton Road soon after four o'clock in the early hours of Monday June 26. Again there was widespread damage although only one person was killed. Twenty-one were seriously injured.

People were growing familiar with the flying bombs. They looked like a small fighter aircraft with short, squared-off wings. The primitive jet engine made a loud, raucous rattling noise, and a spurt of flame was clearly visible coming from the tail. In the nose of the machine was the warhead containing approximately one ton of explosive. The fuel was an ordinary low grade petrol, and when this was all used up the engine stopped and the flying bomb plunged to earth. The sudden silence was generally regarded as 'the worst sound of all', to be followed within seconds by the awful noise of the explosion. The Germans called the flying bomb the Vergeltungs-waffe I or VI (Revenge Weapon Number 1), revenge for the mass bombing of German cities.

On Saturday July 1 Fulham had its worst day of the War for flying bombs. Three fell in the Borough within a period of eight-and-a-half hours. The first was in Avalon Road at half-past-three in the afternoon. Fifteen people were killed and seven seriously injured. An hour later a second flying bomb came down in Mooltan Street. Here there were two fatalities and three people seriously injured. Then just before midnight the third of the flying bombs crashed at the Lewis Trust Buildings in Lisgar Terrace killing seventeen people and seriously injuring thirty-one others. This incident proved to be the worst caused by flying bombs in Fulham. There was extensive damage to property with masses of broken glass and slates off roofs. Many people had to be accommodated in rest centres pending emergency repairs to their homes or the finding of vacant places in Fulham. Looting was becoming a problem again as had been the case during the 'blitz'.

People were leaving London in large numbers. The Government was reluctant to start an official evacuation scheme, partly because the railway system was under great pressure moving men and materials to the embarkation ports for the Continent. Eventually public opinion became strong enough to result in action, and the first organized parties of schoolchildren left London on July 3. Fulham children were included in this movement, and some of them went as far away as Cornwall, South Wales and Yorkshire. A few days later, pregnant women and mothers with small children began to leave. London's main line stations were constantly crowded, except for Charing Cross and Victoria which served Kent and Sussex. Nobody wanted to go there because many flying bombs were being brought down in those areas by R.A.F. fighter aircraft and anti-aircraft batteries.

One result of the exodus from London was that, for a time, food was easier to get. Queues became much shorter and there was a good choice of things on points. Some people returned from shopping in triumph with a tin of sardines. These had seldom been seen in the shops since the early days of the War.

Fulham's seventh flying bomb came down in Reporton Road on July 12 just after half-past-four in the afternoon. Two people were killed and twenty-six seriously injured. Effie Place was the location of the next flying bomb at half-past-five on the morning of July 17. Nobody was killed but fifteen were seriously injured. After that, there was a series of incidents with comparatively few casualties. The Shell Mex Depot in Townmead Road at quarter-past-one in the early hours of July 23 suffered extensive damage, but there were no fatalities and only two seriously injured. A flying bomb in the allotments at Fulham Palace in the afternoon of Friday July 28 injured seven people seriously but nobody died. Shortly before midnight on July 29 the railway track behind Western Hospital in Seagrave Road was badly damaged. Train services to Walham Green were disrupted for the next day or two until repairs were completed. On July 30 a flying bomb fell in the north-west corner of Brompton Cemetery in Kensington. This was close to the Fulham boundary, and caused damage to West Brompton Station and the railway track. In the early hours of July 31 a flying bomb fell on Barnes timber yard in Peterborough Road. There was one fatality and seven seriously injured. The last of the flying bombs in Fulham, and in fact the last incident in the Borough for the entire War, was at Beaumont Crescent at twenty minutes before midnight on Wednesday August 2. Seven people were killed and twenty-seven seriously injured. There was considerable damage.

In addition to the thirteen flying bombs which came down in the Borough, five others crashed into the Thames just before reaching Fulham. Mercifully, they did not have quite enough fuel in their tanks to travel the little extra distance which would have added to the deaths and destruction which had become all too familiar that summer.

At their meeting on August 8, Fulham's Civil Defence Committee received a letter from the Bishop of London thanking them for the assistance given at Fulham Palace after what he referred to as the 'slight incident' there on July 28. He went on to comment on the rescue work he had seen going on in Fulham and wrote: 'It must make all the difference to sorely strained people to have such prompt, thoughtful and sympathetic help brought to them at once. The men of these services are doing a splendid work quite splendidly and I felt I must bear my testimony to it.'

With the coming of the flying bombs, people had quickly got back into the habit of going to the air raid shelters and spending the night in them. Fulham's public air raid shelters could accommodate 8180, and it was estimated that there was an average of five thousand people in them during the flying bomb phase. Canteen facilities were again provided for the larger shelters as had been the case earlier in the War. It all brought back memories of the winter of 1940-41. The Government made more Morrison shelters available and Fulham Council was able to get seven hundred for immediate issue in the Borough. In addition another one hundred Anderson shelters were distributed. It was obviously undesirable that people should gather in crowds so Fulham's entire Holidays at Home programme was cancelled.

There was widespread sympathy in the rest of the country for London's predicament and a general wish to help. One thousand Wardens in provincial towns volunteered to come into London and twenty-five of them were allocated to assist in Fulham. Many building workers were brought in to help with the huge task of repairs. At one time fifty of them were billeted in the Fulham Palace Road School rest centre and another fifty in Munster Road School. Their priority work was to get tarpaulins secured on damaged roofs, but inevitably there was a shortage of tarpaulins. There was also the familiar acute shortage of glass. Many shattered windows had to be covered with a felt material, but this tore easily in windy conditions. It was hoped to get supplies of a composite board to replace the felt, but this took time.

In August there came the welcome news that the Gibraltarians were going home and would be vacating three blocks of North End House. The Government was making this accommodation available for homeless people. One block would be allocated to Fulham Borough Council, one to Hammersmith Borough Council and the third for any adjoining Boroughs who might have serious difficulties in housing people. Many flats in Queens Club Gardens, which had been occupied by staff officers working at St Pauls School, were also becoming vacant. The German defensive line in Normandy had finally broken at the end of July and the Allies were moving forward rapidly. The army staff officers were transferred to France and the vacated flats became available for Fulham's homeless. A map of Normandy showing the positions reached by the Allies when the staff officers transferred to France was left in St Pauls School. It is now displayed in the Montgomery Room in the new St Pauls School at Barnes.

By the beginning of September the launching areas of the flying bombs in North East France had been over-run by the Allied advance. The main phase of the flying bomb attacks then came to an end. There were to be more flying bomb attacks in the ensuing months. Some were launched by aircraft, and some longer range ones were fired from Holland in March 1945. Few reached London. None came to Fulham.

In the middle of September the Fulham Civil Defence Committee received a report on the amount of damage caused by flying bombs in the Borough. The number of houses completely demolished totalled 262, whilst another 457 were so badly damaged as to be uninhabitable. Repairs were in hand on a further 767 which were badly damaged but could be brought back into use, whilst 16,055 had sustained minor damage. Just over six hundred men were at work on repairs. The evacuees were streaming back, sometimes to homes that were far from weatherproof. It was desperately urgent to complete the first-aid repairs before the onset of winter.

In November instructions were received from the Government that the Civil Defence Services were to be reduced by approximately fifty per cent. There was some doubt in Fulham, and in other parts of London, as to the wisdom of this decision. The second of the German Revenge weapons, the V2 long range rocket, had been fired towards England for several weeks. The first rocket to reach London had fallen in Chiswick in the early evening of September 8 and the explosion, said to have been like a sudden loud clap of thunder, had startled people in Fulham. Although only a small number of rockets was reaching London nobody was complacent. The hard experiences of the War years had taught them to be ready for anything.

In November the Fulham Battalion of the Home Guard was demobilised. They assembled in the Regal Cinema at Walham Green on Sunday morning November 19 for a farewell service, after which they were addressed by the Commanding Officer. He spoke of the Battalion's record over the years. A total of 3755 men had passed through their ranks since that summer of 1940. Although the Home Guard had never had to go into action against the enemy, they had maintained a high state of preparedness throughout the War. After the address the Battalion marched to Parsons Green where the Mayor took the salute, before the final command to Stand Down. 'Dad's Army' had gone into honourable retirement.

The winter of 1944-45 was a hard one and there were shortages of coal resulting from the steady run-down of the coal mines during the War years. Some twenty thousand men had been leaving the industry annually either because of age or for health reasons. There had been virtually no intake of new men. In the early weeks of 1945 many Fulham people made their way to the Sands End Gas Works to buy coke from the large dumps there. An old pram was most commonly used for moving the fuel.

With the enemy falling back on all fronts the end of the War could not be long delayed. On May 2 all restrictions on lighting were removed except for some coastal areas. The ending of the blackout was a glorious relief. Small children stayed up late to watch the street lights come on, a sight they had never seen before. On May 7 the Germans signed an instrument of unconditional surrender. VE Day (Victory in Europe) was May 8 and two days national holiday followed. The Mayor of Fulham made an official announcement of the end of the War in Europe from the balcony over the Harwood Road entrance to the Town Hall. The local churches held thanksgiving services in the evening generally to large congregations. The bells could not ring out that night from the medieval tower of All Saints Church as they had at the end of the First World War. The demand for manpower had taken all the ringers away and it was November before the Ringing Master was able to organize a Victory Peal.

Many celebration street tea parties were arranged throughout Fulham, some of them not until early June. A few people decorated the outside of their houses in readiness to welcome home a man in the services. Large signs, such as 'Welcome Home Jack', were to be seen. Jack might well have been away for years and his date of demobilization unknown. It did not matter. The flags and bunting could stay up until he came.

The order to disband the Civil Defence Services soon came and on Sunday July 1 a Stand-Down Parade was held in South Park. All the members of Fulham's Civil Defence Services were invited to take part, including past and present, full-time and part-time. Representative detachments from the Police and the National Fire Service were present. The Mayor took the salute at the march past before the final dispersal. It was an emotional occasion. Some of the older men had answered the call for A.R.P. volunteers in the years before the War and had helped to build up the organization. Their work was now finished, but the memories of their experiences in the bombing would remain with them for the rest of their lives.

Various changes in everyday life were soon in train. Weather forecasts were resumed on the radio. There had been none during the War because the forecasts might have been useful to the enemy. In early June the basic petrol ration for private motoring was restored, and later in the month the weekly ration of tea was increased to 2½ ounces. All static water tanks were drained and their demolition was soon in hand. By the middle of June the children evacuated under the official schemes had all been brought back. In Fulham they were taken to Sherbrooke School which had been chosen as the dispersal point where the evacuees could be reunited with their families.

Items of information began to appear in the local newspapers which had not been mentioned during the War for security reasons. It was reported that maintenance men attached to the Fleet Air Arm had been trained at the Gas Company's Watson House in Sands End. During the last year of the War some eight or nine hundred naval ratings had been billetted at Imperial House in Townmead Road. They had been used as building handymen and were 'coached' all over London to help with house repairs. In order to obtain the maximum production of war material, many women had worked part-time in small engineering works helping to make items of arms equipment. The Power Station in Townmead Road had been an important centre for such work in Fulham. Regular full-time employees formed the nucleus of the labour force but many Fulham women had worked there on a part-time basis.

In May the Coalition Government was brought to an end, and it was decided that a General Election should be held on July 5. All the men and women away in the armed services were to be given the opportunity to vote if their names were on the Register of Electors. An organization had to be set up to bring ballot papers from the far corners of the world. July 26 was agreed as the day on which the votes were to be counted. The election resulted in the biggest electoral landslide since 1906, a Labour Government being returned to power with a large majority. In Fulham East, Michael Stewart was elected and went on to become Fulham's longest-ever serving M.P. In Fulham West, Dr Edith Summerskill was re-elected. Both of them had large majorities.

On August 6 and then on August 9 atomic bombs were dropped, first on Hiroshima and then on Nagasaki. On August 14 the Japanese Government resolved to accept unconditional surrender. Victory over Japan was officially celebrated on September 2 and there were more street parties in Fulham. Many bonfires were lit in the streets but they were all rather on the small side. Fuel shortages meant that there was not much wood available for frivolity. Yet after all the celebrations there was commonly a 'flat' feeling. The War had overshadowed every aspect of life for years. Now the tension and the drama were over and the long haul back to 'normality' was about to begin. It was to take many years.

INDEX

A

Abercrombie, Professor 72
Ackmar Road School 29
Air raid precautions – see Civil Defence
Air Raid Precautions Act 11
Air raid shelters 16, 17, 18, 20, 21, 29, 30, 39, 41, 45, 47, 50, 51, 53, 61, 81
Air raid Wardens 11, 12, 13, 14, 16, 20, 21, 29, 31, 48, 50, 53, 68, 76
Air raid warnings 14, 20
Aliens 26, 34
All Saints Church 34, 82
All Saints School 43
Allotments 54, 62
American soldiers 67, 72
Anti-aircraft guns 38
Anti-aircraft shells 38
Austria 13
Avalon Road 79

B

Babies Hospital, Broomhouse Road 26
Banfield, J.W. 58
Barbers Stores 76
Barons Court Station 38
Barrage Balloons 25, 71
Barton, Councillor P. 71
Basuto Road 47
Battle of Britain 36
Beaumont Crescent 80
Beaumont Mansions 70
Bell, George, Bishop of Chichester 73
Bethnal Green Underground Station 69
Bevin, Ernest 57
Bishops Park 25, 31, 38, 42, 44
Blackout 15, 23, 24, 27, 82
Bomb disposal 40, 75
Bombing: casualties anticipated 1, 15, 20, 22, 23
Brompton Cemetery 80
Brunswick Boys Club 39
Bucklers Alley 39
Buses from provinces 42

C

Canadian soldiers 67
Chamberlain, Neville 16, 24, 25, 32
Chancellors Road 75
Charing Cross Hospital (Fulham) 10
Charleville Road 47
Chelsea and Fulham Railway Station 43
Chipstead Street 68
Churchill, Winston 15, 32, 35, 53
Cinemas 25, 27
Civil Defence:
    Emergency Committee 21, 23
    Council Committee formed 10
    Home Office plans 9, 10, 11
    London Region 20
    Mobilisation 24
    Press criticism 28
    Recruitment 11, 13, 15, 16, 17, 18, 20, 21, 22

Services halved 82
Services disbanded 83
Clothes Rationing 55, 71
Conscientious Objectors 26
Conscription 21, 27, 35
Control Centre 10, 34
Coventry 44
Cromwell Road extension 61
Czechoslovakia 14, 16, 17, 20

— D —

Da Palma, Councillor 10, 11, 45
Dawes Road 77
Dawes Road Congregational Church 77
Daylight saving 41
Decontamination 18
Delvino Road 47
Docks fire 37
Dunkirk Evacuation 33

— E —

Eelbrook Common 25, 39, 58
Effie Place 80
Eridge House Day Nursery 26, 29
Evacuation 19, 23, 28, 31, 35, 47, 80, 83
Everington Street School 29

— F —

Felden Street 75
Fifth Columnists 33
Fire Services 12, 13, 14, 22, 24, 28, 35, 49, 50, 56, 60, 62, 65, 68, 75, 83
First aid services 10, 12, 14, 15, 16, 21, 26, 28, 31, 50, 58, 63
Flying Bombs 79
Food decontamination 72

Food rationing 29, 31, 48, 49, 51, 54, 55, 56, 61, 66, 68, 71, 80
Food waste collection 54
Fuel rationing 65
Fulham Central Library 77
Fulham Central School for Boys 73
Fulham County Secondary School 28, 30
Fulham Hospital 10, 17, 33, 37, 46
Fulham Palace 69, 80
Fulham Palace Road School 43, 44
Fulham Power Station 10, 13, 17, 37, 40, 83
Fulham Registration Records 50
Fulham Secondary School 28, 30
Furniture stores 50

— G —

Gas masks 11, 14, 16, 64, 65
Gas, poison 10, 12, 18, 26, 32, 51, 56, 64, 70
General Election 83
Gentry, Alderman 46
Gibraltarians 36, 81
Glass breakage 22, 64, 68, 70, 76, 79, 81
Gowan Avenue 57
Grand Theatre 74
Green Line Buses 24
Greyhound Road 45

— H —

Halford Road School 26, 28, 44
Hammersmith Railway Station 37, 40
Harwood School 28, 30
Heckfield Place 51
Hitler, Adolf 10, 13, 16, 17, 73
Holidays at Home 61, 78, 81
Home Guard 32, 34, 48, 63, 70, 74, 82
Horder Road 47

Horton, Councillor T. 66
Hurlingham Club 25, 40, 41, 45, 62

I

Incendiary bombs 12, 15, 21, 65, 73
Incident Inquiry Point 76
Iron railings for scrap 58

J

Jervis Road 42

K

Keir Hardie House 37
Kelvedon Hall 44
King George VI 77

L

Lady Margaret School 24, 35, 72
Langford Road School 26, 28, 44
Laski, Harold 9
Lewis Trust Buildings, Lisgar Terrace 79
Lillie Road 47
Lillie Road School 43, 44
Lintaine Grove 78
Looting 42, 79
Lord Haw-Haw 43
Lysia Street 40

M

Magnetic Mines 31
Market Hall 44
Maternity and Child Welfare Centre, Parsons Green 12, 17, 26, 28

Maternity Home, 706 Fulham Road, 12
Melcombe School *see Fulham Palace Road School*
Mooltan Street 79
Mortuaries 26
Mulgrave Road 42
Munich 17, 18
Munster Park Methodist Church 45
Munster Road 38
Munster Road Depot 12
Munster Road School 30
Mussolini 33

N

National Registration 26
National Savings 53, 61, 64, 70, 77
Nella Road 37
New Kings Road 38
North End Road School 74

O

Oil bomb 37

P

Parabomb 74
Parachute mines 42, 45, 52
Parachutists 33
Parsons Green Cricket Club 52
Pearl Harbour 58
Peterborough Road 80
Petrol rationing 30, 62, 83
Phosphorus bombs 74, 75
Place-names removal 34
Poland 22, 23
Purcell Crescent 47
Putney High Street 73

Q

Queens Club 54, 74
Queens Club Gardens 81
Queensmill Road School 25, 30

R

Racton Road 79
Rannoch Road 37, 75
Reporton Road 80
Rescue parties 12, 50, 52
Rivermead Court 45, 74
Rockets 82

S

St Augustine's Church 42
Rosaville Road 75
St Dionis Road 38
St Dunstans Road 37
St Dunstans Road School 30
St James Church Hall 43
St Marys Church 79
St Pauls School 43, 74, 81
Sandbags 11, 17, 23, 24, 31
Sands End Gas Works 13, 39, 40, 41, 55, 75
Settrington Road 73
Shell Mex Depot 75, 80
Sherbrooke School 83
Skelwith Road 75, 77

Sloane Square Underground Station 44
Soap rationing 60
South Park 23, 40, 42
Soviet Union 22, 53, 63, 64
Spanish Civil War 10, 11, 13, 14, 20
Stewart Michael 83
Summerskill, Dr Edith 58, 83

T

Townmead Road 38

U

Unrotated projectiles 75, 77

V

VE Day 82

W

West Brompton Station 80
West Kensington School 28
West London Emergency Secondary School for Girls 31
Western Hospital 31, 33, 80
William Parnell House 41
Windsor: Old Windsor Hospital 24
Womens Voluntary Services 13

Children from Langford Road School evacuated to Cambridge, September 1939.